# GREAT WORDS
## *of the* GOSPEL

*By*

## H. A. IRONSIDE. Litt. D.

## MOODY PRESS
### 153 INSTITUTE PLACE
### CHICAGO, ILLINOIS

# CONTENTS

# PREFACE

The addresses now before the reader were delivered in most part on successive Lord's Day mornings at the Moody Memorial Church, Chicago, Illinois. They were intended especially for confirming the faith of young converts, a number having been brought recently to know Christ as a result of special revival services.

I trust in this permanent form these messages may be used of God to help establish others who have recently come to know Christ as their Lord and Saviour, and that even older believers may find some measure of profit if they will take time to read them thoughtfully.

H. A. Ironside.

# I

# REGENERATION

IN taking up this series of addresses on some of the great words of the gospel, I shall be thinking particularly of babes in Christ, that is, those who only recently have been brought, through the gracious ministry of the Holy Spirit, to a saving knowledge of our Lord Jesus. Babes need to be fed. The apostle Peter says, "As newborn babes, desire the sincere milk of the word, that ye may grow thereby." "Strong meat," we are told elsewhere, "belongeth to those who are of full age." That is, the deeper truths of the Word of God are for Christians who have had years of experience in the ways of the Lord. It is not of such that I am now thinking, but of those who only a little while ago were still in nature's darkness, but have been awakened and saved, and are now, I trust, hungry to learn more of the precious truths of the Word of God.

First of all, I want to talk to you about regeneration. My text is found in Titus 3, verses 3 to 7:

> For we ourselves also were sometimes foolish, disobedient, deceived, serving divers lusts and pleasures, living in malice and envy, hateful, and hating one another. But after that the kindness and love of God our Saviour toward man appeared, not by works of righteousness which we have done, but according to his mercy he saved us, by the washing of regeneration, and renewing of the Holy Ghost; which he shed on us abundantly through Jesus Christ our Saviour; that being justified by his grace, we should be made heirs according to the hope of eternal life.

In this passage we see what we once were, before we were converted. Verse 3 describes the lives we then lived. Verse 4 tells of the marvelous way in which God our

Saviour has intervened. He has revealed Himself to us in the person of our Lord Jesus Christ, through whom we have been justified and made heirs according to the hope of eternal life. Verse 5 tells us of the work that takes place within every converted soul. Altogether apart from human effort, God has saved us by the washing of regeneration and renewing of the Holy Spirit.

It is the word "regeneration" upon which I want you to fix your attention. This word is found only twice in our English Bible, and the original word thus translated is never found anywhere else but in these two instances—here and in Matthew 19, verse 28, where we read: "Ye which have followed me, in the regeneration when the Son of man shall sit in the throne of his glory, ye also shall sit upon twelve thrones, judging the twelve tribes of Israel." The word "regeneration" means a second birth or a new creation. In Matthew, the Lord was speaking of the earth's new birth, when the present distressing circumstances will pass away and new conditions will prevail, at the coming of the Son of man to reign in righteousness over all this lower creation. That will be the time when men shall beat their swords into plowshares and their spears into pruninghooks, and the nations shall learn war no more. Then every man will dwell in peace under his own vine and fig tree. It will be the time when Messiah will be King over all the earth, and rule the nations with the inflexible iron rod of righteousness. That will indeed be earth's regeneration, a new creation, a new condition of things for this poor world.

But in the Epistle to Titus, the only other place where we have the word "regeneration" in the Bible, the reference is to the work that takes place in an individual when he is born again through believing the gospel of our Lord Jesus Christ. Look again at verse 3, where the apostle speaks of our past condition, we who are now regenerate. In those days we were deluded by the devil. Our hearts were filled with unholy desires. We gave ourselves to many things that were displeasing to God and hurtful to ourselves. "We were sometimes foolish," says the apostle. In spite of the fact that we are now regenerate, we are sometimes foolish still. How easily we give way to temptations! How readily we allow ourselves to come under the power of worldly things! But characteristically, the days of our folly ended when we came to Christ. Before that, we were indeed foolish. We were wickedly disobedient, following our own natural, fleshly desires, living unabashed in our sinful ways, dishonoring God's holy name. Many of the evil things to which we gave ourselves obtained power over us because of Satan's deception. He, the arch deceiver, had taken us captive at his will. In those days of our deception, when we thought of the Christian life, it seemed to us anything but desirable. We imagined that Christians must necessarily live very gloomy, unhappy lives, and that the only people who thoroughly enjoyed life were those who lived for the world and its follies.

But now all this is changed. We have been brought to know Christ. This is true of many of you. You heard the voice of God calling you to repentance; you turned to Him, confessing your sin; you trusted the Lord Jesus Christ; you believed the gospel, and you have now become His children through "the washing of regeneration, and renewing of the Holy Ghost."

In the account of our Lord's interview with Nicodemus, as related in the third chapter of John, we are told how he startled that Jewish doctor of the law by declaring that he must be born again, born of water and of the Spirit. Do not make the mistake of supposing that "born of water" means baptismal regeneration. There is no such thing taught in the Word of God. Water, throughout all of John's writings particularly, and also in many other parts of the Bible, is the recognized symbol of the Word of God, and this passage in Titus makes it perfectly clear. The new birth is by the Word and the Spirit. This is the washing of regeneration and renewing of the Holy Spirit.

In John 4, we find the Lord speaking to a poor, sinful woman at the well of Sychar. She was outside the pale of respectability. He knew all about her, about all her failures, but His heart went out to her, and He desired to make of that woman a new creature. He did not talk to her in the same way as He did to Nicodemus. He spoke to her of the unsatisfactory character of all that this world has to offer, and in contrast with that He presented the preciousness of eternal life, and He told her that eternal life would be hers when she received the water that He would give. You remember His words: "Whosoever drinketh of this water shall thirst again: but whosoever drinketh of the water that I shall give him shall never thirst; but the water that I shall give him shall be in him a well of water springing up into everlasting life."

Now, whatever water means here, it means exactly the same in chapter 3, for here we are told that eternal life is received when we drink of the water that Jesus gives, and in John 3 we are said to be born of water and of the Spirit. To be born again and to receive eternal life are really one and the same thing. When we were born naturally, we received natural life; when we were born from above, we received spiritual or eternal life.

The figure that Jesus used is not a new one. That is why Nicodemus should have understood better than he did. In Psalm 119, verse 9, David says, "Wherewithal shall a young man cleanse his way? by taking heed thereto according to thy word." Jeremiah chided the people of Israel in the name of the Lord, saying, "They have forsaken me the fountain of living waters, and hewed them out cisterns, broken cisterns, that can hold no water." Ezekiel tells how God will sprinkle clean water upon those who turn to Him, cleansing them from all their idolatry and their filthiness, and He will take away their stony hearts and give them hearts of flesh. This is what He does when people are born again.

Farther on in this Gospel, the Lord Jesus says, "If any man thirst, let him come unto me and drink." He offers the living water to all who will receive it. In the book of the Revelation we read, "Whosoever will, let him take of the water of life freely." The water of life is the glorious gospel message that comes down from the throne of God and flows out into the deserts of this world, bringing life and healing wherever it goes. In the book of Proverbs we read, "As cold waters to a thirsty soul, so is good news from a far country." That is exactly what the gospel is. The very word means good news, the good news that Christ Jesus came down from heaven to save all poor sinners who will put their trust in Him. This is the living water. Receive it, take it into your heart, and you will be born of water and of the Spirit.

And with this agree the words of the apostle James. He says in James, chapter one and verse 18, "Of his own will begat he us with the word of truth, that we should be a kind of firstfruits of his creatures." How are we begotten? By the Word, the Word of truth. Then the apostle Peter tells us the same thing. He says, "Being born again, not of corruptible seed, but of incorruptible, by the word of God, which liveth and abideth for ever. For all flesh is as grass, and all the glory of man as the flower of grass. The grass withereth, and the flower thereof falleth away:

but the word of the Lord endureth for ever. And this is the word which by the gospel is preached unto you" (I Peter 1:23-25). There it is. James says we are begotten of the Word; Peter says we are born again by the Word of God which liveth and abideth forever. And so, believing the Word, we receive the living Word. It is the Word that the Spirit of God used in order to produce the new life.

When we are born again, we are cleansed from our old sins, so the thought of washing is also connected with the Word. Think again of the passage I quoted from the one hundred and nineteenth Psalm: "Wherewithal shall a young man cleanse his way? by taking heed thereto according to thy word." As we walk in obedience to the Word of God we are kept clean and free from the defiling things of this world. This, too, is what Ezekiel emphasized in chapter 36, verses 25 to 27:

> Then will I sprinkle clean water upon you, and ye shall be clean: from all your filthiness, and from all your idols, will I cleanse you. A new heart also will I give you, and a new spirit will I put within you: and I will take away the stony heart out of your flesh, and I will give you an heart of flesh. And I will put my spirit within you, and cause you to walk in my statutes, and ye shall keep my judgments, and do them.

This should all have been clear to Nicodemus, but he failed to understand it. Then in Ephesians, chapter five and verses 25, 26, we read:

> Christ also loved the church, and gave himself for it; that he might sanctify and cleanse it with the washing of water by the word.

So it is by the Word that we are born again and by the Word we are washed. The old things that were once so dishonoring to God are washed out of our lives when we trust in Christ. We should never again be characterized by our former habits and behavior.

Do not forget that new birth is something more than just accepting certain doctrines. It is receiving Christ and believing the gospel, as a result of which we are created anew in Christ Jesus, and we receive eternal life with all its new and godlike desires. God expects of you who have trusted Christ something different from what was found in your lives in the old days before you were saved. Old habits should disappear, and they will if you let the Spirit of God have His way in your life. Do not be discouraged because you find you do not become perfect immediately. No Christian is perfect, but we are all going on to perfection. Those of us who have been converted many years have to say with Paul, "Not as though I had already attained, either were already perfect: but I follow after, if that I may apprehend that for which also I am apprehended of Christ Jesus." When you are converted, the Holy Spirit of God begins His work of renewal, and it goes on all through life—the renewing of the mind. The Spirit of God uses the Word, as we meditate upon it, so that our hearts' desires are changed, and more and more we come to understand His will. As we walk in obedience to that will, we grow in grace, and in the knowledge of our Lord and Saviour Jesus Christ.

We may see from this how important it is that we daily study the Word of God and spend time before Him in prayer, looking to Him to open up His truth and apply it to our own hearts and consciences. If we are consistent and persistent in thus seeking to know the mind of the Lord, our lives will be transformed as the Holy Spirit works in and through us, giving the Word as we need it for our food, and using it too as water for the cleansing of our ways.

Before the blessed Lord went home to heaven, He promised that the Holy Spirit would come to carry on the work that He had begun, and when He took His place at the right hand of the Father, as Peter says, "He hath shed forth this, which ye now see and hear." He was referring to the Holy Spirit, who was acting in such mighty power on the day of Pentecost. He is the blessed Comforter who has now come to indwell each believer, and as we yield ourselves to His guidance, we are enabled to live lives of victory and to enjoy fellowship with our Father in heaven.

Do not be content, dear young convert, in days to come, just to look back and say, "So many years ago on such and such an occasion I was born again." Do not be forever thinking of that happy day when Jesus washed your sins away. It is all right to sing that beautiful hymn. I love to sing it, too, but I do not want to have to look back to all my happy days. Every day ought to be a happy day, and will be if we go on in fellowship with God. "The path of the just is as the shining light, that shineth more and more unto the perfect day." As you let the Spirit of God have His way in your life you will be conscious of the renewing of the Holy Ghost, changing your affections and desires, fixing your mind and heart on things above.

# II

# REDEMPTION

LET us now consider the second great word: Redemption. This comes before us in the first Epistle of Peter, chapter 1, verses 18 to 21.

> Forasmuch as ye know that ye were not redeemed with corruptible things, as silver and gold, from your vain conversation received by tradition from your fathers; but with the precious blood of Christ, as of a lamb without blemish and without spot: who verily was foreordained before the foundation of the world, but was manifest in these last times for you. Who by him do believe in God, that raised him up from the dead, and gave him glory; that your faith and hope might be in God.

The word "redemption" is one that runs all through the Bible; in fact, we can say without any suggestion of hyperbole that it is the great outstanding theme of Holy Scripture. This important truth runs through the Book like the proverbial red strand that, we are told, runs through the cordage of the British navy. Everywhere, from Genesis right on to Revelation, you find God in one way or another presenting to us the truth of redemption—redemption in promise and in type in the Old Testament; redemption in glorious fulfillment in the New Testament.

What do we mean when we use the term "redemption"? Ordinarily, and in Scripture too, the word means to buy back, to repurchase something that has been temporarily forfeited; or, it means to set free, to liberate, as we speak of redeeming one from slavery; or, it means to deliver, as to redeem one from some grave danger.

Back there in Israel in olden times, if a man fell into

difficult circumstances, found himself burdened with debt, he might mortgage his entire property, and if that was not enough to satisfy the claims of his creditors, he could even mortgage his own strength, and ability, his own physical powers. He could sell himself into a kind of slavery until his debt was paid. Sometimes, he found himself hopelessly thus enslaved. Scripture says, however, "After that he is sold, he may be redeemed again." One of his brethren may redeem him, or, if he is able, he may redeem himself. It would be almost impossible in most instances for anyone to redeem himself. Probably, the only way would be if he suddenly fell heir to some vast estate. But on the other hand, if he had a rich relative who cared enough for him to undertake to meet the liabilities and discharge them, he might thus be set free.

The one who did this was called a kinsman redeemer, and he was a wonderful type of our Lord Jesus Christ. The Hebrew word is *goel*. He comes before us in Scripture long before the time of Israel. Even in the book of Job you read of him. It was of the *goel* that Job spake when he said, "I know that my redeemer liveth, and that he shall stand at the latter day upon the earth."

Then one may, as I say, have forfeited his property. Well, some wealthy one could come and pay off the mortgage and thus redeem the property. We are used to such transactions today, and we attach that meaning to the word "redemption."

Now, in thinking of man, we know he is a sinner, sold under judgment. It was his own fault. God says in His Word, "You have sold yourselves for naught; and ye shall be redeemed without money." It is not possible for any man to redeem himself from the sad condition in which he finds himself because of sin, but that is why we need a kinsman redeemer who is more than man, one who is divine as well as human.

When we turn to consider this subject of redemption in the New Testament, we find it presented in three different ways: first, redemption from judgment. That is redemption from the guilt of sin, which is through the atoning work of our Lord Jesus Christ. But that is not all. It is not only the will of God that we should be redeemed from the judgment due to sin, but Scripture has a great deal to say about redemption from the power of sin, so that we might be redeemed from those evil habits and unholy ways which at one time held sway over our lives. This redemption is through the indwelling Christ, through the risen Christ working in the power of the Holy Spirit, who makes Christ real to His people down here.

And then Scripture speaks of a third aspect of redemption: the redemption of the body. I have been redeemed as far as my soul is concerned, if I am a believer in the Lord Jesus Christ. I am daily being redeemed from sin's power, if I am walking in subjection to the Holy Spirit's guidance. But though I am thus redeemed in measure, I am made to realize every day that this very body of mine is often a hindrance instead of a help in regard to my practical deliverance; but I am looking forward to the time when the body itself shall be redeemed and made like unto the glorious body of our Lord Jesus Christ. Then I shall be redeemed from the very presence of sin and from all the evidences of its corruption.

Here in the first Epistle of Peter, the apostle carries our minds back to a wonderful event that took place in the land of Egypt centuries before, that event which the Jewish people to this day celebrate annually in the Feast of the Passover. The Israelites were slaves in Egypt, suffering under Pharaoh's cruelty, and God, you remember, said, "I have come down to deliver thee," and He told Moses of something that was to take place whereby, He says, "I will put a difference (or literally, a redemption) between my people and the Egyptians." That redemption was made by the blood of the passover lamb; and it is to this that the apostle Peter is referring typically in his first Epistle when he says, "Ye were not redeemed with corruptible things, as silver and gold, from your vain conversation (empty behavior) received by tradition from your fathers (ancestrally handed down); but with the precious blood of Christ, as of a lamb without blemish and without spot" (literal rendering).

God gave directions to Israel through Moses for every household to seek out a lamb, and they had to be very careful as to their choice of a lamb. There must be nothing about it that marred it in any way, as it was to be a type of Christ, God's holy, spotless Son. There must be no blemish of any kind, either outwardly or inwardly. This lamb had to die, and then they were to take the blood that was shed and caught in a basin, and sprinkle it upon the lintel and the two side posts of the door of the house wherein they dwelt. And God commanded them to go into the house and shut the door, for He had declared that He would pass through the land of Egypt that night, and smite all the firstborn, but wherever the sprinkled blood was seen, the firstborn and all the family would be secure, for Jehovah said, "When I see the blood, I will pass over you."

The blood of the lamb shed so long ago was God's picture of the blood of the Lord Jesus Christ which was shed on Calvary's cross fifteen hundred years later, but to which we now look through the mists of nearly two thousand years. How can that blood avail for our redemption to-day? The blood had to be sprinkled of old on the actual lintel and door posts and then they were safe inside. It is centuries since Christ has died. In what sense, then, can we be made secure from judgment through the blood that He shed so long ago?

We read in the Epistle to the Hebrews of having our hearts sprinkled by the blood of Christ. How is that blood applied to our hearts? Through simple faith. In the Epistle to the Romans, chapter 3, after dwelling on the lost condition of all men by nature and practice, the apostle says in verse 23 and on, "For all have sinned, and come short of the glory of God"; and then adds: "Being justified freely by his grace through the redemption that is in Christ Jesus: whom God hath set forth to be a propitiation through faith in his blood, to declare his righteousness for the remission of sins that are past, through the forbearance of God; to declare, I say, at this time his righteousness: that he might be just, and the justifier of him which believeth in Jesus" (Romans 3:23-26). What is he telling us? That the sacrifice of the Lord Jesus is all-availing, that it is sufficient for all men everywhere, that it settled for the sins of all men in past ages, who looked on to the cross in faith, and it settles now for all in the present age and in all the years to come, who look back to that cross in faith—"through faith in his blood."

In other words, when we trust the One who shed His blood at Calvary, then we are numbered amongst those who have redemption through the sacrifice that He offered, and that means that we are secure forever from the judgment due to sin, just as Israel, sheltered beneath the blood of the passover lamb, was secure from the judgment that was to fall upon Egypt, for God said, "When I see the blood,

I will pass over you." So today, we who put our trust in the Lord Jesus Christ are redeemed from the judgment that is hanging over this poor world—the judgment that sin deserves. And so we can enter into the meaning of that scripture which says, "There is therefore now no condemnation to them which are in Christ Jesus."

Some of you have only lately come to Christ; you have not known the Lord very long. Oh, I beg of you, do get this clear. Your salvation, your security from judgment does not depend on anything that you can be or do. It depends upon the work that the Lord Jesus did for you on Calvary, the redemptive work that He accomplished when He suffered in your place upon the Tree, and you enter into the good of that redemption through faith in Him. When Satan comes to tempt you, when you discover things in your own heart that you did not realize were there, just meet him with this: the redemption that is in Christ Jesus has settled everything, has made me free, has given me deliverance from the judgment of a holy God.

The believer is said to be redeemed from the curse of the law. He was exposed to that curse because of sin. God has declared, "Cursed is every one that continueth not in all things which are written in the book of the law to do them." We have failed; we have broken God's law; we are under that curse. But our blessed Redeemer was made a curse for us, as it is written, "Cursed is every one that hangeth on a tree." Redemption guarantees our safety from judgment.

When we turn to the Epistle to Titus, we have another aspect of redemption. In chapter 2, verses 11-14, we read:

> For the grace of God that bringeth salvation hath appeared to all men, teaching us that, denying ungodliness and worldly lusts, we should live soberly, righteously, and godly, in this

present world: looking for that blessed hope, and the glorious appearing of the great God and our Saviour Jesus Christ; who gave himself for us, that he might redeem us from all iniquity, and purify unto himself a peculiar people, zealous of good works.

It cannot be too often insisted upon that salvation is not of works, lest anyone should boast, that no works of ours could avail for our redemption; but here in this message we have another side of the truth emphasized, and that is that our blessed Lord not only died to redeem us from the judgment due to our sins, but He died to redeem us from all iniquity, that is, from all lawlessness. And sin is lawlessness. He died, as Mrs. Alexander's beautiful old hymn puts it, not only to save our souls, but "He died to make us good." The gospel has not accomplished its purpose if it only frees people from judgment. It has not completed its work until it presents every believer in the glory, fully conformed to the image of God's blessed Son.

We have been called to holiness, to purity of life, to uprightness of behavior, and if any of us who profess the name of Christ are playing fast and loose with unholy things with worldliness, with carnality, with impurity, with things that defile these temples of the living God, these bodies in which the Holy Spirit dwells; if we are in any way living so as to bring dishonor upon the name of the One who died to save us, we are just to that extent thwarting one of the purposes for which Christ died. He died to redeem us from all iniquity. Here the word "redemption" is used in the sense of deliverance. He died to deliver us from all iniquity, to draw us away from the evil things that peril our Christian experience and that would wreck and ruin our lives.

Redemption was illustrated in a stirring news article that appeared in our daily papers recently. Many read the story of those men shipwrecked in the South Pacific in connection with the world war. A number of them were huddled upon a raft and only one of them was able to swim, and he a big, burly colored man. When those sailors saw nothing but death and despair before them, this colored man sprang into the sea and towed that raft as he swam for over six miles through shark-infested waters, until he brought them all to a place of safety. That was redemption, and that man was a redeemer.

Our Lord Jesus not only risked His life, but gave His life, not only to save us from judgment, but also to "redeem us from all iniquity, and purify unto himself a peculiar people, zealous of good works." Dear young Christian, I beg of you, do not allow yourself to be careless as to this aspect of redemption. Do not be content to know that you have trusted Christ as your Saviour from hell, and forget that you are called upon to live a heavenly life here upon this earth. Do not be content to say that at a given time or at a certain meeting you went into an inquiry room and told the Lord Jesus you would trust Him as your Saviour. Remember that in doing that you received Him not only as the Saviour of your soul but as the One who is to be Lord of your life, the One who died to redeem you from everything that is unholy.

We read, "Who gave himself for us, that he might redeem us from all iniquity, and purify unto himself a peculiar people, zealous of good works." Do not let it ever be said of you that you are not concerned about good works, and do not ever tell people that because salvation is not of works, it does not matter what kind of lives they live. Our Lord Jesus Christ says, "Let your light so shine before men, that they may see your good works, and glorify your Father which is in heaven." They cannot see your faith, but they can see your works, and if your life is not in accordance with your faith, they will soon realize it and will put you down as a fraud and a hypocrite, and instead of your influence being for good, it will be for evil.

James says in his Epistle, "Thou hast faith, and I have works: shew me thy faith without thy works, and I will shew thee my faith by my works." You cannot show your faith without works, and so in that sense faith without works is dead. Justification is by faith, absolutely without works, but the same scripture that tells us that, puts emphasis on our works as the evidence of our salvation. In the Epistle to the Ephesians, chapter 2, we read: "For by grace are ye saved through faith; and that not of yourselves: it is the gift of God: not of works, lest any man should boast." But Paul immediately adds, "For we are his workmanship, created in Christ Jesus unto good works, which God hath before ordained that we should walk in them." That is our practical redemption. If one scripture tells me that "this is a faithful saying, and worthy of all acceptation, that Christ Jesus came into the world to save sinners; of whom I am chief"; another Scripture says, "This is a faithful saying, and these things I will that thou affirm constantly, that they which have believed in God might be careful to maintain good works." Our Lord Jesus, the living Saviour, has sent His Holy Spirit to dwell within us, in order that as we walk in the Spirit we may find this practical redemption from the power of evil in the life.

But there is a third aspect of redemption, and that is brought before us in the eighth chapter of the Epistle to the Romans. In verse 22 we read: "For we know that the whole creation groaneth and travaileth in pain together until now. And not only they, but ourselves also, which have the firstfruits of the Spirit, even we ourselves groan within ourselves, waiting for the adoption, to wit, the redemption of our body." "We ourselves groan within ourselves." Of whom is he talking? Christians. Groaning Christians? Yes! Oh, I thought Christians were always happy; I thought they were always shouting and singing! Well, you have a lot to learn. Thank God, it is possible to joy even in the midst of sorrow, and Christians have their griefs and sorrows and trials. But they have a wonderful Saviour to carry them through those trials—One to sustain and help them in every hour of distress.

One of our chief causes of groaning is that of physical infirmities, and that is what the apostle is talking about here. In our unconverted days our groaning was caused by our sins. We cried out in pain as we longed for deliverance. Then we were groaning in bondage. Now as Christians we groan in grace, because of physical infirmities that are often such a hindrance in our lives. Perhaps you were just getting ready to go to prayer meeting one night. (I hope you love the prayer meeting.) But you did not get there. You were preparing to go, when suddenly you came down with such a sick headache that you had to stay at home. When others were gathered for prayer and praise, there you were, lying on the couch sniffing at camphor, and you were saying to yourself, "What a wonderful day it will be when I get a new body and a new head that will never ache." Well, that is what the apostle means when he says, "We that are in his body do groan." We are so often hindered by physical weakness, but we are looking on to the day of the redemption of the body. We have the firstfruits of the Spirit, but we are looking forward to the full "son placing," for that is what the word "adoption" means. Then we shall be fully conformed to the Son of God.

When will that be? In Philippians, chapter 3, verse 20, we read, "For our conversation is in heaven; from whence also we look for the Saviour, the Lord Jesus Christ: who shall change our vile body." When our Bible was translated, the word "vile" did not mean something wicked and corrupt, but it meant something of a humiliating character, and so this might be translated, "Who shall change the body of our humiliation, that it may be fashioned like unto his glorious body, according to the working whereby he is able even to subdue all things unto himself." He is drawing our attention to that wonderful event which should now be the hope of the Christian, and I am thinking again of you young Christians. He wants you now to get before your soul as the lodestar, the blessed hope of the Lord's return. The One who died for you on the cross is coming again, and He is coming to receive you to be with Himself. He could not have you there in the glory as you now are. "Flesh and blood cannot inherit the kingdom of God." So in order that you might be suited for the place to which He is going to take you, He will give you a new body, a glorified body; and when you receive that, you will be fit for a place in the Father's house.

He said before He went away, "I go to prepare a place for you. And if I go and prepare a place for you, I will come again, and receive you unto myself; that where I am, there ye may be also." And we learn from other scriptures what will take place in order to prepare us for the Father's house. The first Epistle to the Thessalonians, chapter 4, is a wonderful passage as to this. It says, "The Lord himself shall descend from heaven with a shout, with the voice of the archangel, and with the trump of God: and the dead in Christ shall rise first: then we which are alive and remain shall be caught up together with them in the clouds, to meet the Lord in the air." That is the time when the body will be changed, and our redemption will be complete. Already we have the redemption of the soul; we have been redeemed from judgment. We are experiencing day by day, as we walk in obedience to the Lord, practical redemption, redemption from the power of sin. When our blessed Saviour returns, our redemption will be complete—spirit and soul and body will be fully conformed to the image of our Lord Jesus Christ.

# III

## SUBSTITUTION

THE word I now desire to bring before you is one that is not actually in the Bible. It is the word "substitution." Although it is not in the Bible, it stands for a great truth that runs through the Scriptures from Genesis to Revelation. That is, the fact that the Lord Jesus Christ in infinite grace took the place of poor, lost, guilty sinners, and made it possible for a holy God to reach out in mercy and save all who would come to Him in the name of His beloved Son.

I do not have one particular text in mind, but I have been thinking of five different passages in the New Testament where we get the same expression—He "gave himself"; and I want you to think with me of these scriptures. The One who gave Himself was our Lord Jesus Christ, and I should like you to notice what it was for which He gave Himself.

In the Epistle to the Galatians, chapter 2 and verse 20, the apostle Paul writes:

> I am crucified with Christ: nevertheless I live; yet not I, but Christ liveth in me: and the life which I now live in the flesh I live by the faith of the Son of God, who loved me, and gave himself for me.

Note the individuality of it. Paul, who had been a bitter persecutor of the people of God, who had been an enemy of the Cross of Christ, one day had his eyes opened, and he suddenly realized that the One who died on that cross went there for him, that He had taken his place, that it was love that led Him to go to that shameful death. From that moment the heart of Saul of Tarsus went out in ador-

ing gratitude to our Lord Jesus Christ, and until the very
end of his days he found his greatest joy in trying to give
some evidence, by a life of service, of his love for the One
who had thus loved him.

Notice how he speaks of Him: "The Son of God, who
loved me, and gave himself for me." There you have the
very heart of the Gospel—"Himself for me." That is substitution. Some people tell us, because we do not find the
actual word "substitution" in the Bible, that the truth of it,
the fact of it is not there, and so they talk of atonement
by other means than by substitution, atonement by example
or atonement by reconciling love, that leads men to turn
to God adoringly, simply because of the goodness that He
showed in seeking them out in the person of His Son.
But no, the Word of God makes it very definite. The work
that took place on Calvary was a substitutionary trans-
action. It was the Lord Jesus Christ, God's own blessed,
eternal Son, who became man for our redemption, giving
Himself on our behalf.

"The Son of God loved me, and gave himself for me."
That is the language of faith. When a poor, needy sinner
looks at that Cross and sees, as it were, the blessed Saviour
hanging there, he says, "He was there for me; it was my
sins that put Him there; it was in order that I might be
fitted for the presence of God that He went into the darkness and endured the judgment of God. He is my Substitute. The Son of God loved me, and gave Himself
for me."

But it is not only for me, it is also for us. In the Epistle
to the Ephesians, chapter 5 and verse 2, we read:

> And walk in love, as Christ also hath loved us, and hath
> given himself for us an offering and a sacrifice to God for a
> sweetsmelling savour.

I am so thankful that in my thinking I do not have to limit the gift of God's grace in the person of His Son to just some little group, as though it were just for a small elect company that Jesus died. "He gave himself for us." I can look out over the whole wide world, whether men are saved or unsaved, and say to them on the authority of the Word of God that "He gave himself for us"—for everyone of us. Whether you be Jew or Gentile, whether you be very religious or have no time for religion, I would say to you, "The Son of God gave himself for us." He saw us in our lost condition, and He went to Calvary's cross in order to redeem us. That is how the Prophet Isaiah puts it. He looked on down through the centuries and by faith he saw the very scene of Calvary, and he cried out, "He was wounded for our transgressions, he was bruised for our iniquities: the chastisement of our peace was upon him; and with his stripes we are healed."

I remember a number of years ago I went over to a town in Minnesota to hold some meetings. My wife and our eldest son, just a little child at the time, went with me. When we got there, a big, burly highland Scotsman met us. He said, "Now you come along with me; I am going to take you to my house. We are going to sleep you there, and then across the way at the McKenzies they will eat you." Of course I knew he didn't mean anything cannibalistic, and I was glad to accept the provision made. We went to his house and settled ourselves, and then went over to the McKenzies for our meal.

I remember one Sunday we left to go down to the meeting in the afternoon, and it happened that there was one daughter in the family who had not yet received the Lord Jesus Christ as her Saviour. The mother said, "Will you pray for Jean? She knows the way, but somehow she doesn't seem to want to come. She says she is young yet

and she wants to have her fling before she settles down."
Well, we did pray for her, and some way or other as I
preached that afternoon in the big tent, I couldn't help
seeing Jean way in the back, eagerly listening to the message. When it was over, I thought she might be one who
would move to the front when the invitation was given,
but instead of that, I saw her get up and hurry away, and
I felt a little bit disappointed. When I finished speaking
with those who had come forward, I went on home, and
when I got there I found, as I opened the front door, my
wife sitting there with an open Bible and Jean beside her.
My wife turned to me and said, "Come and join us. I am
trying to show Jean that Christ died in our place, but some
way or other she can't seem to grasp it." So I sat down
with them and said something like this: "Jean, you know
the gospel, don't you?"

"Yes," she said, "I think I do."

"What is the gospel?"

"Well, it is that Christ died for our sins according to the
scriptures"; and my wife said, "I have been showing her
Isaiah 53." The Bible was open at that chapter so I said,
"Look, you have it right here: 'But he was wounded for
our transgressions, he was bruised for our iniquities: the
chastisement of our peace was upon him; and with his
stripes we are healed.' Don't you see, Jean? Christ died
for you, He took your place, He bore God's judgment
against your sins."

"I see what is written there," she replied, "but somehow
I can't get hold of it for myself. It doesn't seem to
mean me."

So we got down on our knees and prayed that the Spirit
of God Himself might make the great truth of the substitutionary work of the Cross real to her; and then I said to
her, "Jean, while we are here on our knees, I want you

to read the Words for yourself, and we will pray that the Holy Spirit will open them up to you." And so she read them: "But he was wounded for our transgressions, he was bruised for our iniquities: the chastisement of our peace was upon him; and with his stripes we are healed."

Then she said, "Yes, I see it, but I don't seem to be able to make it my own."

"Perhaps it would be different now if you will just read it again and change the pronoun, putting it into the first person singular. Read it like this: 'He was wounded for *my* transgressions'; because you see, Jean, it really means that. He was wounded for the transgressions of all of us, yours and mine. Read it that way." And she started to read, "He was wounded for *my* transgressions." She stopped as the tears began to flow. She wiped them away and read on, "He was bruised for *my* iniquities," and again she stopped; and then she read, "The chastisement of *my* peace was upon Him," and then she fairly shouted, "Oh, I see it! With His stripes *I am* healed." And in a moment the light had shone into her darkened heart. She saw that the Lord Jesus was *her* substitute; He had taken *her* place. We gave thanks, and then she said that she must go and tell her "Mither." She didn't know that all the while her mother had been standing outside the window and had heard the whole thing. Out the front door she went and down the garden path and around to the side, and she ran right into that mother's arms. "Oh Mither, Mither, I'm saved; by His stripes *I am* healed." What joy that brought to the mother's heart, and what a happy time of rejoicing we all had then!

You see, that is substitution. That is the very pith and marrow of the gospel. A poor old colored woman was asked once, "Dinah, you are always talking about being saved through the atonement of Christ, but do you know what the word 'atonement' means?" She looked up and said, "Honey, 'deed ah does understand de word 'atonement.' It just means this: He die, or me die. He die, so me no die." "The Son of God loved me, and gave Himself for me." He gave Himself for our sins.

Next we do have a special group mentioned for whom He gave Himself. In the last part of the fifth chapter of Ephesians, in the twenty-fifth verse we read:

> Husbands, love your wives, even as Christ also loved the church, and gave himself for it.

When we get home to Glory, when we who have been redeemed to God by His precious blood are presented faultless in the presence of our heavenly Bridegroom, we shall look up into His face and we shall be able to say, "The Son of God loved the Church, and gave Himself for it."

You remember the story that is told of one of the generals of Cyrus the Great, king of Persia, and the one who overthrew, in God's providence, the mighty Babylonian Empire. One of his generals came home from a campaign and was shocked to find that in his absence his own wife had been arrested and was languishing in prison, charged with treachery against her country, and the trial was to be held that very day. The general hastened to the court of Cyrus, and the guards brought in his own beloved wife. She, poor woman, pale and anxious, tried to answer the charges brought against her, but all to no avail. Her husband, standing near, heard the stern voice of the Persian ruler pronounce the death sentence. In a moment, as they were about to drag her away to behead her, he ran forward and threw himself down at the feet of the Emperor. "Oh sire," he cried, "not she, but me. Let me give my life for hers. Put me to death, but spare my wife." And as Cyrus looked down upon him, he was so touched by his deep devotion and his love for his wife that his heart was softened. He remembered, too, how faithful this servant had been, and he gave command that the wife should go free. She was fully pardoned. As her husband led her out of the room, he said to her, "Did you notice the kind look in the eyes of the Emperor as he pronounced the word of pardon?" She said, "I did not see the face of the Emperor. The only face that I could see was that of the man who was willing to die for me."

Oh, when we get home, when we see the face of the Man who did die for us, how our hearts will praise Him! How we will rejoice in His presence as we say, "The Son of God loved me, and gave Himself for me."

We need to realize that He died not only to deliver us from the judgment due to our sins, but He died for us in order that we might be delivered from the power and polution of sins right here and now in this life. In Galatians 1:4, we have these words:

> Our Lord Jesus Christ, who gave himself for our sins, that he might deliver us from this present evil world, according to the will of God and our Father.

He gave Himself for our sins, not simply that we might have our past sins forgiven, nor that we might stand justified before Him as to the future, but in order that the power of sin might be broken in our lives, that we might no longer be subject to Satan's authority, that we might be free men and women, living here to the glory of the Lord Jesus.

This is one of those truths that I do want to press upon you who have but recently been brought to a saving knowledge of Christ. Dear young Christian, do not be satisfied to know that you are saved from hell, blessed as that is, but oh, go on day by day to a fuller walk with God, that you may be saved from sin, and that your whole life may be lived to His praise and to His glory.

After all, somebody might raise the question, "Well, it is perfectly true that it says He gave Himself for us, and He gave Himself for the Church, and He gave Himself for our sins; but are you really sure that it applies to everybody? May He not, after all, have had just some particular elect company in view when He thus gave Himself, and if we do not belong to that company, what right have we to come to Him at all, and to expect Him to do anything for us?" For answer, will you look at the first Epistle to Timothy, chapter 2, verses 5 and 6:

> For there is one God, and one mediator between God and men, the man Christ Jesus; who gave himself a ransom for all, to be testified in due time.

Oh, dear friends, do not allow anything to narrow down your conception of the inclusiveness of the work of our Lord Jesus Christ. "He gave Himself a ransom for *all.*" Do not try to read into that what it does not say. Some people say, "Well, of course, you know we must understand the words 'the elect' to come in there. He gave Himself a ransom for all the elect." Oh no, God does not need you and me to help Him out. He knows what to say, and He means what He says. When He writes, "He gave Himself a ransom for all," He means us to understand the words exactly as they are written.

They used to tell a story about a certain professor of theology at Princeton Seminary in the days when Princeton was pretty rigid as to what they called "a limited atonement." One day one of the students looked up and said, "Professor, just what is our stand in this seminary on the atonement?" And the teacher replied, "Well, we stand with Dr. ———; we preach the theology of Dr. ———, and he taught a limited atonement—that Christ died only for the elect." Then said the student, "And over at New Haven, Connecticut, (at that time New Haven was a very sound seminary,) what do they teach there? What is Dr. Taylor's theology?" The professor said, "Over there they teach that God so loved the world, that He gave His only begotten Son, that whosoever believeth in Him should not perish, but have everlasting life."

"Oh," said the student, "well, I'll accept that because that is what the Bible says. That is not just Dr. Taylor's theology or New Haven doctrine; that is the Word of God."

And so we say to you, whoever you may be, the Lord Jesus gave Himself a ransom for *all*. On Calvary's cross He put away sin by the sacrifice of Himself. In other words, when He presented Himself there as a substitute for guilty humanity, He finished the work that satisfied every righteous demand of the Throne of God and met all the claims of His holy nature, so that on the basis of it, any poor sinner in all the world who comes to Christ and puts in his claim will be saved on the basis of the substitutionary work of our Lord Jesus Christ. That is the doctrine of the atonement as we have it in the Bible. There is no other in this blessed Book, and so we put the question to you: have you put in your claim? There are a lot of people who know all about it, but they have never believed and acted upon it.

You remember the incident of the veteran of the Civil War who was found living in wretched poverty. The city authorities found him in such a deplorable state that they thought all they could do was to take him to the county poor farm. One of them happened to notice something on the wall. It wasn't exactly a picture; it looked more like a document of some kind. He took it down and looked at it, then he asked, "What is this, my friend?" The poor old man replied, "That was sent to me by Abraham Lincoln himself, and I kept it because it has his signature on it." It turned out to be a check. I forget the amount of money, but it was really a pension check signed by the President and sent to this man years ago. Instead of cashing it, the poor man had kept it all the time, and had framed it and hung it there on the wall. In the meantime he got poorer and poorer, until he was a candidate for the county farm. They found that the government at Washington would still honor the check, although it was years old, and so they had enough to take care of the man comfortably until he died.

Oh, do not be content just to have the statement of the substitutionary work of the Lord Jesus, but come to Him for yourself, trust Him as your own Saviour. Cash in on it. He gave Himself a ransom for *all.*

# IV

## JUSTIFICATION

Be it known unto you therefore, men and brethren, that through this man is preached unto you the forgiveness of sins: and by him all that believe are justified from all things, from which ye could not be justified by the law of Moses (Acts 13:38, 39).

JUSTIFICATION! It is a big word, and very often people miss its true meaning. What is it to be justified? It is to be cleared of all blame, to be freed from every charge. It is the sentence of the court in favor of the prisoner. The prisoner stands there, charged with certain things; the evidence is all heard, and the jury brings in a verdict of "Not guilty." The man is justified.

Notice a most remarkable thing in these two verses. We have two things here which God does for the believing sinner that no man could do for anyone else. You could not both forgive a man and justify him at the same time. If you forgive him, he cannot be justified. He must be guilty, and therefore there is something to forgive. On the other hand, if you justify him, then you do not need to forgive him. Suppose, for instance, one had been charged with a certain crime, and after everything had been heard, the jury says, "Not guilty," and the judge pronounces him free. As that man comes out of the courtroom, a friend says to him, "It was kind of the judge to forgive you, wasn't it?" The man replies, "He did not forgive me; I did not require his forgiveness. I was justified; I was proven not guilty and did not need to be forgiven."

Of course, human judges may sometimes make a mistake. You have heard the story of the colored brother who was arrested, charged with stealing a gold watch and

chain. After all the evidence of the complaining witness
had been heard, the judge looked down at the prisoner
and announced, "The sentence of this court is acquittal."
The man leaned forward and said, "What was that you
said, judge?"

"I said, the sentence of the court is acquittal."

The colored man looked puzzled, and said to the judge,
"Judge, ah don' jist undahstan' what dat means."

"Well," the judge explained, "I mean you are acquitted."

"Well, judge, does that mean I gotta give the watch
back?"

You see, the man was guilty, and the judge himself had
been deceived.

But God will never be deceived. Nobody can ever put
anything over on Him. He knows every sin that you and
I have ever been guilty of—sins in thought, sins in word,
and sins in deed; and then in addition to all of these, sins
of omission. Failure to do the things that we know we
ought to do is just as truly sin as to commit overt acts of
evil. And God knows all about it, and "all have sinned,
and come short of the glory of God." "There is not a just
man upon earth, that doeth good, and sinneth not."

But God undertakes both to forgive the sin and to justify
the sinner; to clear him of every charge, when he puts his
trust in His blessed Son, our Lord Jesus Christ. You could
not do that for anyone, but God can and He does it
because the Lord Jesus Christ in infinite grace conde-
scended to take our place, to bear the judgment that our sins
deserved, so that when we come to God confessing our sins,
over against all that sin and over against all that wicked-
ness stands the finished work of the Lord Jesus Christ.
And on the basis of that, God says, "I forgive this man,
and accept him before my presence as though he had never
sinned at all. I count him as righteous, and justify him

fully and completely." That is the meaning of justification.

You who have just recently come to trust the Saviour, I wonder if you have entered into that. I wonder if you realize that the moment you trusted the Saviour, that instant God gave you a new standing before Him. You stand before Him now as if you had never sinned at all. You say, "Well, I can't forget my sins. They come up before me when I lie down at night; they come before me when I kneel to pray; and they are before me even in the daytime. There are so many things that I wish had never happened, and I sometimes wonder, since they come crowding in upon my mind as they do, whether they are really forgiven."

Let me assure you, if you have really trusted Christ, they are not only forgiven, but forgotten. God says, "Your sins and iniquities will I remember no more," and if God has forgotten them, then you and I may well say, "I too will seek to forget, and say with Paul, 'Forgetting those things which are behind, . . . I press toward the mark for the prize of the high calling of God in Christ Jesus'."

God Himself is the author of our justification. We read in the Epistle to the Romans, chapter 8, and really in one sense I am beginning at the wrong end; I am beginning where God leaves off here in the Epistle to the Romans, but I am beginning where I think you and I as sinners need to begin. In Romans 8 we read that it is God Himself who justifies. Take verse 33:

Who shall lay anything to the charge of God's elect? It is God that justifieth.

We are justified by God, the source of it. It is He who has taken up this question, who has gone into it fully and completely, and He says, "Now I am satisfied to acknowledge as righteous the man who trusts my blessed Son."

Some years ago a friend of mine, a French evangelist,

Paul J. Loizeaux, was preaching in a certain place, and somebody came to him one day and said, "Could you come and see a woman who is very sick? We are afraid she is dying. She is troubled about her soul and doesn't seem to understand the way." Of course he gladly went, as any of us would under such circumstances. As he entered the room and sat down beside the bed, the woman said, "Tell me what is necessary in order that my soul may be saved and my sins forgiven." He told her the old, old story, the story of the Cross. He told her how God commendeth His love toward us in that while we were yet sinners Christ died for us. He told her how, hanging on that cross in those awful hours of darkness, our blessed Lord Jesus, as the substitute for sinners, drank the cup of wrath that we deserved, and made full satisfaction for iniquity; and now God can justify everyone that believes in Him, whom He raised from the dead.

When he finished, she said, "Oh yes, I know, I understand all that, but I don't see how I can know that my sins are forgiven." So again, very patiently, he went over the same story, but tried to present it in a little different light. He told her that the Lord Jesus was the one great sacrifice for sin, that He offered Himself for our sins; that He was made sin for us, He who knew no sin, that we might be made the righteousness of God in Him. And when he finished, she said, "Yes, I understand that, but is that all that is required?"

The evangelist sprang from his seat. He was a very fiery man by nature, and sometimes the fire came out even after he became a Christian. He said in a tone that shook the room, "You wicked woman!"

And she, lying there so sick, was almost terrified, and said to him, "Oh, sir, why do you talk to me like that?"

"You wicked woman, you vile woman! You ask me

what is necessary in order that you may be saved. I tell you how God has bankrupted heaven to save your guilty soul. I tell you how He has sent His own blessed Son to give His life for you. I tell you how He was forsaken of God upon that Tree, and you have the insolence to look up into the very face of God and say, 'Is that all?' What more would you want? It is all that God Himself could do."

She burst into tears and exclaimed, "Oh, sir, I understand. I did not realize what I was saying. Oh, I thank God for what He has done. It is enough! If it is enough for God, it surely is enough for me!"

Oh, that is it! The Lord Jesus Christ gave Himself. "He loved me, and gave himself for me." God sent Him. God saw you and me in our deep, deep need, and He sent Him to die for us, and now it is God that justifies the ungodly. God justifies whom? The ungodly. Oh, I thought He justifies the godly, the good, the pure, the true, and the noble! No, God justifies poor, lost, guilty sinners when they "believe on him that raised up Jesus our Lord from the dead; who was delivered for our offences, and was raised again for our justification" (Rom. 4:24, 25). It is our faith in the Word of God and the work of Christ that is counted for righteousness. Read Romans 4:5, "But to him that worketh not, but believeth on him that justifieth the ungodly, his faith is counted for righteousness." The basis of it all is given in Romans 5:9, where we read, beginning with verse 8:

> But God commendeth his love toward us, in that, while we were yet sinners, Christ died for us. Much more then, being now justified by his blood, we shall be saved from wrath through him.

Notice three things here. First, we who believe are now justified. It is not that we may, as some people put it, have a good hope of salvation, that we may hope that we shall be justified at last, that we may hope that in the day of judgment everything will be all right; but we are *now* justified—every believer in Christ. Oh, so many of our hymns were written by people who hadn't full assurance of salvation, and they express so often the desire that they may be cleansed and justified. How many real believers sing, "Wash me and I shall be whiter than snow!" And yet everyone who has truly trusted the Lord Jesus Christ is already washed, made white by the blood of the Lord Jesus, justified by God.

What is the basis of justification? His blood! It is because of what He did. It is because of the blood He shed—the shedding of His precious blood; it is the giving up of His life. It is His life for ours; His holy, spotless life over against our sinful, wicked lives. The Son of God loved me, and gave Himself for me.

Somebody might say, "Well, I just do not understand what you mean. You talk about being justified by blood. In what sense could one be justified or cleansed by blood?" Let me give you an illustration. Out in the state of Washington, at the time of the first World War, four or five convicts in some way or another got over the wall of the penitentiary and escaped. After several weeks they were all captured, except one who was never located, at least not until the circumstances which I am going the mention. He was able to get away, and eventually under an assumed name he joined the army. After a period of training he was sent across to France. One day, however, some other soldiers were added to the number, and one of them looked at this man and said, "I remember him. I knew him back in the state of Washington years ago. That's so-and-so. He is not going by his right name. I remember when he was condemned to the penitentiary for burglary." He went to the officer in charge and told him what he knew about the man. The officer in turn wrote to the War Department and asked, "What am I to do with this man? He is an escaped convict." Washington sent word back to arrest him and return him to America as a prisoner. But in the meantime something had happened which made that impossible.

One night a number of men were wanted for a very, very dangerous duty, and the Captain said, "I am not going to ask any man to do the thing that I am going to tell you about, but I hope that some of you will volunteer. I want some men to crawl out in the dark across No Man's Land and find out what the foe is planning to do. It is a very dangerous undertaking—you may not get back—so I am not going to appoint anyone, but will ask for volunteers." Four men stepped right out, and among them was this convict. Under cover of darkness they crawled out over No Man's Land. There were shells falling all around them, but three of them got through safely. The fourth man, the convict, apparently had got clear through to the enemy and secured the information and was coming back, when a shell fell and burst so near him that he was killed. They brought his mangled body in and when the officer received the word from Washington to return that man a prisoner to this country, the officer wrote back, "He has washed out his crimes in his own blood." He had given himself, he had given his life, and the giving of his life had washed out his crime against the government, though of course this did not touch the question of his sin against God.

The Lord Jesus Christ was absolutely without offence. He was the holy Son of God, but He looked upon us poor sinners in our deep need and He took our place in judgment. He went to the Cross and He bore what our sins deserved. He poured out His life in the shedding of His

precious blood, and when we receive Him we can say that
He has washed out our sins in His precious blood. He had
no sins of His own for which to die. He was there for
our sins.

> Oh, why was He there as the Bearer of sin,
>  If on Jesus thy guilt was not laid?
> Oh, why from His side flowed the sin-cleansing blood,
>  If His dying thy debt has not paid?

He took your place. Have you trusted Him? Do you
believe God's sure promise? If you have, you are justified
by His blood.

"Well," you say, "on what principle does God thus justify?" The Epistle to the Romans, chapter 3 and verse 24,
tells us:

> Being justified freely by his grace through the redemption
> that is in Christ Jesus.

God justifies men by grace, not because of merit. You
and I had no merit. Everything was against us. Demerit
was ours, and no merit did we have to plead. But now God
says in grace, "I am ready to take up that man and save
him, if he will but receive and confess my Son as his
Lord." It is so hard for people to understand this. Men
always seem to get the idea that they must do something
in order to merit God's favor. It would not be grace if it
were merited. Grace is unmerited favor, and it is favor
to those who have merited the very opposite. That is grace.

Suppose, just to use a very hackneyed illustration, that
my sons were still school boys and there is a rowdy, a
regular bully in the neighborhood, and he falls upon one
or the other of them and knocks him down and steals his
books and his lunchbasket, and then when I go out to
talk to him, this bully turns on me and strikes me and
stones my house, breaking my best plate-glass window. I
have every reason to be thoroughly provoked with him.

I would have a perfect right, you know, to go to the police and have him arrested and charged with assault and battery, and one thing or another. But suppose instead of that I wait, and on some cold winter day I happen to see that young rowdy, and, as I am watching, I see him fall in the snow, and I run out after him. I learn that he has had no one to care for him. He is an orphan, and has no father or mother to look after him, and I find he staggered and fell because of lack of food, he was so weak. When he sees me coming, he staggers to his feet and tries to run away. But he cannot get away because I have hold of his arm. He looks up at me and pleads, "I'll never do it again, if you will let me go." But I say, "You won't get away." I bring him into my own home, warm him up, feed him, and give him a suit of clothes belonging to one of my sons. I take care of him and show him every kindness. He can't understand it, but his heart is won. This is grace. He merited the very opposite, did he not?

Grace is favor shown to the undeserving. If people deserved it, it would not be favor; and so you cannot deserve God's salvation. Often when I say to somebody, "I hope you are on your way to heaven," I receive the reply, "Well, I am doing my best to get there." It is not a question of doing your best. It is a question of receiving the grace of God as manifested in Christ Jesus.

I was very much struck by an incident which I heard our friend Dr. Chafer relate. He was riding in a train going down from Kansas City to Dallas, and they were getting near to Fort Worth when he realized that he had not spoken a word to the porter about his soul. He always tries to be conscientious about speaking to those who serve him and wait upon him in restaurants, hotels, and trains. So he went to look for the porter and found him just finishing up the last of the shoes he had to shine. He sat down there beside him and said, "May I ask you a question?" "Yessuh," replied the porter, "what's your question?" So Dr. Chafer asked him, "How good does a man have to be to get to heaven?"

"Well, I can't tell you just how good a man has to be, but ah knows he has to be mighty good," he replied.

"Well, do you ever expect to get to heaven?"

"I don't know. I've jist about give up tryin'. I've tried and tried fer a long time but it don't seem to do no good, and I'm afraid I'll never make it."

Then Dr. Chafer asked the porter, "Where do you check in? at Kansas City or Forth Worth?"

"I have to check in at the Pullman office at Fort Worth half hour after the train pulls in."

"Oh, I see," said Dr. Chafer. "This train is due at Fort Worth at eight o'clock, and you should check in by eight thirty. Well, we're late now; we'll never make it to Fort Worth by eight o'clock. Aren't you afraid that you are going to be pretty late this morning? Don't you think that you'd better get off at the next stop and start running for Fort Worth?"

The porter looked at him and said, "Why sir, what you talkin' about? You trying t'make a fool out of me? I never could make Fort Worth running for it as quick as I can make it by staying right on this train. I just trusts the man that runs the train to get me there."

And Dr. Chafer said, "My dear fellow, that is exactly how I am going to heaven. 'It is not of him that willeth, nor of him that runneth, but of God that showeth mercy,' and I am trusting the One who runs the Gospel train, the Lord Jesus Christ, and He is going to get me there. I never could get there through any goodness of my own."

The porter looked at him in amazement and said, "Tell me a little more about this. I never heard anything like this before." Dr. Chafer explained the way of salvation to him, and then left a little booklet and a Gospel with him.

About six months later Dr. Chafer was again riding from Kansas City to Dallas, and again the thought came to him that he must speak to the porter. When he found him, he asked him the same question: "How good does a man have to be to get to heaven?" The porter looked at him and grinned, "You're not going to catch me twice on that. You're the man that asked me that question about six months ago. Well, I looked up all those scriptures you showed to me and I'll tell you, sir, I just found there wasn't anything I could ever do to get to heaven, no matter how good I tried to be, so I am trusting Him who loved me and died for me, and I'm telling others about Him, and I know now my soul is saved." Well, that's it—"Being justified freely by his grace through the redemption that is in Christ Jesus."

But how do you make it your own? In what way is it applied to you individually? We read in Romans 5:1, "Therefore being justified by faith, we have peace with God through our Lord Jesus Christ." Justified by faith! What is faith? The little boy was asked by his Sunday school teacher, "What is faith?" He lisped a little, so in reply he stuttered, "Pleathe, teacher, I think ith-juth-believing-God-and-athking-no-quethtionth." That is it. Faith is believing God and not asking any questions. It is taking God at His word. God says, "I am satisfied with the work which my Son has done. Because of that work, I raised Him from the dead and now offer to justify any poor sinner who comes to me in my Son's name and trusts in Him." If you have come, you have a right to say: "Being justified by faith, I have peace with God [everything settled between me and God] through our Lord Jesus Christ." Have you said it? If not, say it now. "The word is nigh thee, even in thy mouth, and in thy heart: that is, the word of faith, which we preach" (Rom. 10:8).

The resurrection of Christ, you know, is the declaration, the seal of it all. In the previous verses, at the end of the fourth chapter of Romans, we read, beginning with verse 22: "And therefore it was imputed to him for righteousness." That is, when Abraham believed God, it [his faith] was imputed to him for righteousness. And then we read:

Now it was not written for his sake alone, that it was imputed to him; but for us also, to whom it shall be imputed, if we believe on him that raised up Jesus our Lord from the dead; who was delivered for our offences, and was raised again for our justification (Romans 4:23-25).

That is justification by His resurrection. Why? Because His resurrection tells of God's satisfaction in the work that His Son has done. When He hung upon that Cross He was bearing our sins, He was taking our place, dying there in the sinner's stead. Now, if He had never come out of that tomb, it would show that redemption was never accomplished. If that tomb remained sealed and the body of Jesus remained in it, then it would show that it was all a farce, and I would not dare to trust Him as my Saviour at all. But see, it is the third day, and His resurrection is the divine declaration that all who believe on Him and rely on Him are justified from all things.

But I know that some of you have been saying in your hearts, or thinking subconsciously at least, "Yes, but there is another side to it. Doesn't the Bible say somewhere that faith without works is dead?" Yes, it does, for we read, "Ye see then how that by works a man is justified, and not by faith only."

"Well," someone asks, "does not that contradict what you have been telling us?"

Not at all. You need to see exactly what it is that various writers of the Epistles are dwelling on. The apostle Paul, and practically all of our references have been from his writings, is telling how poor sinners may be justified before God. But now we turn over to the Epistle of James to find out how we who have professed to believe in Christ may be justified before men.

Suppose I say to my companions in the world, "I have just come to Christ, and I am justified from all things." They have a right to look at me, at my life, to see for themselves whether there is any change in my life. You see, in order to be justified before them, in order to be justified before men, I have to manifest by my good works the fact that I have received a new and a divine nature. Let me read it to you.

> What doth it profit, my brethren, though a man say he hath faith, and have not works? can faith save him? (James 2:14).

That is, what kind of a faith? a faith that has no works? Where there is real faith in Christ one's work will be different. His life will never again be what it used to be. Everything will be changed.

> If a brother or sister be naked, and destitute of daily food, and one of you say unto them, Depart in peace, be ye warmed and filled; notwithstanding ye give them not those things which are needful to the body; what doth it profit? Even so faith, if it hath not works, is dead, being alone (James 2:15-17).

Real faith is manifested by your works.

> Yea, a man may say, Thou hast faith, and I have works: shew me thy faith without thy works, and I will show thee my faith by my works (v. 18).

I cannot show my faith without works, but I can show my faith by my works. If I put my faith in Christ and have trusted Him as my Saviour, I have been justified before God, justified freely, justified for nothing, justified without cost, through the redemption that is in Christ Jesus. Now as I live for the One who has justified me, as I devote my redeemed life to the glory of the One who has saved me, my confession is justified before men. Men who get to know me will say, "That man is real; that man is genuine; he lives what he professes." Do they say that of you? Does your life testify to the reality of the faith that you profess? If you have trusted Christ, you are complete in Him, you are justified freely by His grace. Now by a life devoted to His interests you are to prove to those around you the reality of that faith of which you speak.

# V

# SANCTIFICATION

IN the first chapter of I Corinthians, verse 30, there are some words that I wish to use as a starting point for our consideration of another great word of the gospel.

But of him are ye in Christ Jesus, who of God is made unto us wisdom, and righteousness, and sanctification, and redemption.

It is that word "sanctification" which I desire to emphasize. It is a wonderful thing to know the blessedness of regeneration, to realize that we are saved through an accomplished redemption, to be assured of our justification; and then that leads us on to ask, "What is meant by the believer's sanctification?"

There are a great many different ideas prevalent among evangelical Christians as to the real meaning of the term "sanctification." Some take it to refer to a very definite second work of grace, as they put it, whereby the one who has already been justified is later on, by making a complete surrender of himself to the will of the Lord, completely delivered from indwelling sin, his whole nature cleansed from indwelling sin, so that he no longer has any inward tendency to evil to hinder him in his Christian life.

Then there are others who, while refusing that view, have the idea that sanctification is the gradual improvement of the old nature, bringing it eventually into full harmony with God. I think, as we turn to various scriptures, we shall see that neither of these views is set forth in the Word of God, but that sanctification is something very different from either of them.

The word itself means to be separated; separation, ordinarily speaking, for a holy purpose. You go back to the

Old Testament and it is surprising the variety of things that are said to be sanctified. In the first place we read that God sanctified the seventh day. He recognized the holiness of the seventh day, when He rested from all His work. Then the priesthood in Israel was sanctified, set apart to God. Mount Sinai, where the law was given, was said to be sanctified, for there God in a very special way manifested Himself. The people of Israel were called to sanctify themselves by outward purification, by submitting to certain washings and cleansings, which could not of course affect the state of the heart before Him, but only the cleansing of the body.

There is one scripture in the Old Testament where we read of people being sanctified to do iniquity. That is rather a puzzling holiness. In the last chapter of the book of the prophet Isaiah and the seventeenth verse, the Spirit of God, speaking through the prophet, says: "They that sanctify themselves, and purify themselves in the gardens behind one tree in the midst, eating swine's flesh, and the abomination, and the mouse, shall be consumed together, saith the LORD." Here were people sanctified to unclean practises, sanctified to do things which were abominable in the sight of God, but which were in accord with the practice of heathendom. They were sanctified in this sense to idolatry, so that the word itself really means separation.

Our Lord Jesus was sanctified. "Say ye of him, whom the Father hath sanctified, and sent into the world, Thou blasphemest; because I said, I am the Son of God?" (John 10:36). The Lord Jesus was always the infinitely holy One, but He was the one person of the Godhead who was separated and sent to the world for a special purpose. The apostle Peter says, "Sanctify the Lord God in your hearts: and be ready always to give an answer to every man that asketh you a reason of the hope that is in you" (I Peter

3:15). That is, let God have His place in your heart; let your hearts be separated unto Him.

I want to look at "sanctification" then from three standpoints. First, we read in the Word of God of sanctification by the Spirit; second, of sanctification by the blood of Christ; and third, of sanctification by the Word of God.

First, then, sanctification by the Holy Spirit (Rom. 15:16). Paul asks the Christians at Rome to pray for him as he ministers Jesus Christ to the Gentiles: "Ministering the gospel of God, that the offering up of the Gentiles might be acceptable, being sanctified by the Holy Ghost." In old times the Jewish nation was a sanctified people. That people had been separated from the Gentiles to Jehovah. But now the Gentiles as such are said to be sanctified by the Holy Spirit. That is, as one goes to the nations preaching the gospel, it is the Holy Spirit who prepares people to receive that gospel.

In the second chapter of II Thessalonians this comes out very clearly, verse 13:

> But we are bound to give thanks alway to God for you, brethren beloved of the Lord, because God hath from the beginning chosen you to salvation through sanctification of the Spirit and belief of the truth.

· Notice the order there: Sanctification of the Spirit, then belief of the truth. One might say definitely that no one would ever believe the word of the truth of the gospel, unless he were first sanctified by the Holy Spirit. In other words, it is the Holy Spirit who works in the hearts and minds of people, preparing them for the reception of the gospel. That is why we who go forth to preach the gospel should spend much time in prayer before we appear in public to present the Word, asking God to prepare the hearts of our hearers that the Word may be as seed sown in good soil. That preparation of the heart which is from the Lord is the sanctification of the Spirit here referred to.

In the sixth chapter of I Corinthians, verse 11, after having told of the wicked lives that unsaved men and women live, the apostle says,

> And such were some of you: but ye are washed, but ye are sanctified, but ye are justified in the name of the Lord Jesus, and by the Spirit of our God.

Notice the order there: washed, sanctified, justified. That is, the Word of God is applied to the heart and conscience for cleansing; the Holy Spirit arouses the man, sets him apart from the mass of mankind, makes him ready to receive the Word; and receiving the Word, he is justified.

I remember a great many years ago I was asked to preach in a mission in San Francisco. I sat there for half an hour, listening to some wonderful testimonies, testimonies such as you may hear in the missions of any city, men who had been down and out, telling how God had come in and given them a new life, made new creatures of them. I was so stirred that when I rose up to preach, I changed my subject altogether and I took this text: "Such were some of you: but ye are washed, but ye are sanctified, but ye are justified in the name of the Lord Jesus, and by the Spirit of our God."

At the close of the meeting a rather melancholy looking, cadaverous brother came up to see me, and beckoned me down to the front of the platform. When I went over to him, he said, "My friend, you had your theology all mixed up tonight."

"Oh, is that so?" I asked. "Set me right then, for I do not want my theology to be mixed."

"Yes," he replied, "you put sanctification before justification. No man can ever be sanctified until he is first justified. Justification is the first blessing, sanctification is the second blessing, and you had it turned upside down."

"Oh," I said, "pardon me, I did not make a mistake like that."

"Oh, but you did; you put sanctification before justification."

"Oh, no," I said, "I did not do that. It was the apostle Paul who did that, guided by the Holy Spirit. It was he who wrote: 'Such were some of you: but ye are washed, but ye are sanctified, but ye are justified in the name of the Lord Jesus, and by the Spirit of our God.'"

"No, no," he said, "you are all wrong; you are misquoting the scripture."

"Well," I said, "look at it." I handed him the Bible, and he started to read: "'Such were some of you: but ye are washed, but ye are sanctified, but ye are justi . . .' Wait a minute, there's a misprint here. Let me get my own Bible." So he went back to his seat and got his Bible, came back, and started to read: "'But ye are washed, but ye are sanctified, but ye are justified.' Does anyone have a Revised Version?" he asked. Someone had, and he turned to it and read the same thing. "Well," he said, "that's the first time that I have ever noticed that, but one thing is sure; the apostle Paul wasn't clear on the holiness question when he wrote that." He would rather condemn an inspired apostle than give up his pet theory.

There you have it in the Word of God: "Ye are washed, but ye are sanctified, but ye are justified in the name of the Lord Jesus, and by the Spirit of our God." As I have said before, I am speaking particularly to young Christians. You remember only a few weeks or months ago, many of you did not care anything about the things of God. You were entirely occupied with the things of the world. Then you remember how a change began to take place. You found yourself restless, unhappy, troubled, perplexed, burdened by a sense of sin, a longing to get right with God.

That was not the work of man. It was the work of the Holy Spirit of God, sanctifying, separating you from the world, and preparing you to receive the gospel. Then when you heard the gospel preached in the power of the Holy Spirit, your eager soul drank it in; you believed the truth and you were justified. You were made right with God.

The apostle Peter suggests the same thing in his first Epistle, chapter 1, verse 2, "Through sanctification of the Spirit, unto obedience and sprinkling of the blood of Jesus Christ." When is a poor sinner justified before God? When in the obedience of faith he takes his place beneath the sprinkled blood, like the Israelites of old who entered the house where the blood was sprinkled upon the doorpost and the lintel. But what is it that leads a man to come thus in faith to trust in the shed blood of the Lord Jesus Christ? It is the sanctifying work of the Holy Spirit. This is one aspect of sanctification that begins before a man comes to a saving knowledge of Christ. It is a preparatory work, and then the Spirit of God brings the Word home in power, the man believes it and is justified, and now all through his life afterward the Holy Spirit continues the work of practical sanctification, weaning that man's heart more and more away from the world, and occupying him more and more with a risen Christ at God's right hand. As we are taken up with Christ, as our eyes are fixed upon Him, we become like unto Him, and that is practical sanctification.

But there is another aspect of sanctification, found particularly in the Epistle to the Hebrews. In the thirteenth chapter and the twelfth verse we find these words:

> Wherefore Jesus also, that he might sanctify the people with his own blood, suffered without the gate.

Here we have sanctification by the blood of Christ. What is this? It is the setting apart of the believer in the Lord Jesus to God in all the value of the atoning work of His beloved Son. In the tenth chapter of this Epistle we are told how our blessed Lord went to the cross and there offered one sacrifice for sin, a sacrifice never to be repeated. We sometimes hear of a priest standing at an altar, offering a continual and unbloody sacrifice for the sins of the living and the dead. There is nothing like that anywhere in Scripture. Our Lord Jesus Christ by one offering, settled the sin question, and no other sin-offering will ever be needed. He has taken His seat now at the right hand of God, having accomplished the will of the Father in settling the sin question on the cross, and we read in the tenth verse of this tenth chapter:

By the which will we are sanctified through the offering of the body of Jesus Christ once for all.

That is, we who have trusted that Saviour are now set apart to God. We no longer belong to a world that is under judgment. We are now children of God. We are redeemed to Him by the precious blood of His Son. We are separated to Himself in all the value of His vicarious atonement.

If you look a little farther down in this chapter, at verse 14, you find this remarkable statement, a statement that some of us would not dare believe if it were not found in our Bibles, given by inspiration of the Holy Spirit:

For by one offering he hath perfected for ever them that are sanctified.

Do you believe that? There you have sanctification in its absolute sense. The believer in the Lord Jesus Christ stands before God complete in Christ, perfected forever. No charge can ever be brought against him again. His sins are put away; as far as the east is from the west his transgressions have been removed from him, and he now is in Christ, who is made unto him "wisdom, and righteousness, and sanctification, and redemption."

This is the sanctification that the apostle Paul referred to when he spoke of his call to the ministry, when the Lord said to him, "I am sending you out to proclaim the things that I have already made known to you and that which is yet to be revealed, that you may go to men to open their eyes, to turn them from darkness to light, and from the power of Satan unto God, that they may receive forgiveness of sins and an inheritance among them which are sanctified by faith in Christ Jesus." You can't add anything to that sanctification.. You cannot improve it and, thank God, you cannot take anything from it. It is perfect. It is complete. That sanctification is by the blood of Jesus.

Then there is a third aspect of sanctification. In the seventeenth chapter of John's Gospel we hear our blessed Lord speaking to the Father, engaged in intercession for His own, and He says, in verses 17 to 19:

> Sanctify them through thy truth: thy word is truth. As thou hast sent me into the world, even so have I also sent them into the world. And for their sakes I sanctify myself, that they also might be sanctified through the truth.

He who has already been sanctified by the blood of Christ, set apart to God in all the value of Christ's finished work, is now called upon to walk in this world in holiness of life, a life of practical sanctification, daily being separated more and more from the things that defile, the things that are unclean, the things that are contrary to the mind of God. And this practical aspect of sanctification is by the Word of God.

In Ephesians 5, verses 25 and 26, we read:

> Christ also loved the church, and gave himself for it; that he might sanctify and cleanse it with the washing of water by the word.

You and I then as Christians, and again I say I speak particularly to young Christians, need to familiarize ourselves with the Word of God. We need to give much time to pondering over what God has told us in this blessed Book. David asks, "Wherewithal shall a young man cleanse his way?" and he answers, "By taking heed thereto according to thy word." The Word of God is for our practical sanctification. This is the agency that the Holy Spirit uses in conforming us to Christ.

I trust you see what I mean. You are reading the Bible, and you come across a passage that condemns something that you have been doing for some time. You had not thought of it before. It had never struck you that there was anything wrong in this particular line of behavior, but you are reading something in the Word. "Oh," you say, "I am wrong there. I must never go on like that any more." And so you go to God and confess the wrong, and then you look to Him for grace to glorify Him in that thing.

I knew a man who was converted, and for some time after he was converted he was a heavy smoker. I know I am getting on dangerous ground here, but I am not saying what you should do. I am merely telling you of his experience, and you can draw your own conclusion. He was an earnest Christian but a heavy smoker. One day he was pondering over his Bible. He was reading these words, "Let us cleanse ourselves from all filthiness of the flesh and spirit, perfecting holiness in the fear of God" (II Cor. 7:1). Now I do not know what you would think of that verse in connection with the use of tobacco, but it just went home to his heart. He said, "Here I have brought with me out of Egypt a filthy habit that I acquired when I was a poor sinner down there in sin and bondage." He went right to a shelf in his room and took down a box of cigars, a can of tobacco, and an old pipe, and threw them all into the fire. He said, "I am through with these. I want to be clean because I belong to the Lord Jesus Christ." That was what God did for that man. It would be pretty hard for some of you women who are listening to me, but the Lord is able to deliver you from the cigarette habit, if you will yield yourself to Him in sincerity. And so, whatever it is that God's Word shows you to be wrong, you judge that thing and confess it before God, and as you do you will find deliverance from it.

Thus you are being sanctified by the truth, and you can see from this standpoint that it would never do to claim that you are wholly sanctified. If you are thinking of *positional* sanctification, sanctification by the blood of Christ, yes, you are perfectly sanctified. You could not be any more sanctified than you are. But if you are thinking of *practical* sanctification, no one should ever dare to say that he is wholly sanctified until he gets home to heaven, where he will never more be in contact with sin. You see I might be perfectly sure today that I am walking in the will of God as He has revealed it to me. Tomorrow, as I meditate on some portion of His Word, He might show me something in my life that has been displeasing to Him all along. Then, of course, I kneel before Him and confess it. My sanctification goes on, you see—progressively.

And so then, when we think of sanctification, we think of separation, and we are called to that, to be a people set apart to God. We are set apart by the work of the Holy Spirit drawing us to Christ. We are set apart eternally by the precious blood that has redeemed us; and day by day we are being cleansed and separated from the things that are contrary to the mind of God, as we learn His will through His Word and walk in obedience to it.

# VI

## INTERCESSION

OPEN your Bible, please, at the seventh chapter of Hebrews, and read from verse 24 through verse 27.

> But this man, because he continueth ever, hath an unchangeable priesthood. Wherefore he is able also to save them to the uttermost that come unto God by him, seeing he ever liveth to make intercession for them. For such an high priest became us, who is holy, harmless, undefiled, separate from sinners, and made higher than the heavens; who needeth not daily, as those high priests, to offer up sacrifice, first for his own sins, and then for the people's: for this he did once, when he offered up himself.

We have been considering various aspects of the work of our salvation and now I want to ask you to look with me at the subject of intercession. When I use the term "intercession," I am thinking not only of the intercession of our blessed Lord Jesus Christ at God's right hand, but also of the intercession of the Holy Spirit, who dwells in the hearts of all the people of God while they are down here in this world, and also of the intercession of believers one for another, and on behalf of a needy world.

First, of course, and most important of all is the intercession of our Lord Jesus Christ. We often speak, and rightly speak, of the finished work of Christ. When we use that expression we are thinking of the work whereby the sin question was settled to the divine satisfaction. When the Lord Jesus in infinite grace went to the Cross, there to do the will of God in giving Himself a ransom for our souls, He cried, "It is finished"; and that tells us that as far as the work of saving the soul is concerned there is nothing that we can do.

I remember reading long years ago of a man who lived in Germany in the Middle Ages, who had lived a wicked, reckless life. He belonged to a noble family and had plenty of money, but had used his means extravagantly and in a godless way until at last he was reduced to poverty, and he was filled with remorse as he looked back over his life. He realized that he had not only sinned against himself and his family, but he had sinned against God, and he was anxious to do something in order to make some kind of atonement for his sins. He heard of a certain monastery where they observed a very, very strict routine. Absolute silence was required of the monks who were in the monastery, and only one was permitted to speak to outside people who might come to the gate of the monastery. These monks were given to severe penance. They fasted often, prayed at various hours of the day and night, slept amongst the most uncomfortable of conditions, and in every way were seeking to appease God because of the sins that they had committed. He felt that if he were to enter that monastery and give himself to penance such as that for the rest of his life, he might be able to atone for the sins of the past. So he decided to offer himself as a candidate to become a monk in the monastery.

He had a long way to go but he decided to walk rather than to obtain some means of transportation, thinking that that in itself would be a penance. Finally, footsore and weary, he arrived one evening at the gate of the monastery and knocked and waited. By and by he heard the feeble steps of an aged man coming to the door. The monk opened the upper part of the door — it was one of those double doors that are in two parts—peered out into the twilight, and asked what the visitor wanted. He replied, "I have come to do whatever I can in order to do penance for my sins, in order to appease God and find forgiveness.

I would like to enter this monastery, and I wish you would tell me what I can do in order to put away my sins and make amends for them."

The old monk looked at him and said, "My son, there is nothing left that you can do."

"Oh, is it as hopeless as that?" the man replied. "Have I sinned so much that there is no mercy for me? I am willing to do any kind of penance that the abbot of the monastery may place upon me. I am ready to suffer in any way in order to make atonement for my sins and be prepared for heaven."

Again the old monk answered, "But, my son, there is nothing left for you to do." Bitterly he reproached himself for having waited so long, until now it was absolutely hopeless; and then the monk looked at him again and said, "My son, many years ago as a young man I came to this monastery, actuated by the same feelings as yours. I struggled and toiled and endured all kinds of penances for years, but I found no peace. I had no sense of forgiveness. My heart reproached me, my conscience condemned me. But one day I found here in the monastery a copy of God's Word. It was in Latin, but fortunately I was able to read it, and as I read that blessed Book, God's message to lost man was made known to me. I learned that all that had to be done to make satisfaction for sin had already been accomplished by Christ on Calvary. When He said, 'It is finished,' He meant that there was nothing left that a poor sinner had to do; so I rested in Christ's finished work. Many years have gone by since that day. I would have left the monastery and gone elsewhere, but I have no home on earth—all the members of my family are dead—so I remain here and help serve my brothers, and try as opportunity is given to point others to the blessed Word of God."

As the monk thus ministered the precious gospel of the

grace of God to that poor soul at last he exclaimed, "Oh, I see it! Christ has done it all; there is nothing left for me to do!" Yes, that is it! The work that saves is finished, and you cannot add anything to His finished work. Simply receive and confess the One who bore your sins in His own body on the tree; believe His Word and do not doubt. "Being justified by faith,' we have peace with God through our Lord Jesus Christ."

But while we delight to speak, and rightfully speak, of the finished work of Christ, it is just as correct and it is just as scriptural to speak of the unfinished work of Christ, for when our Lord Jesus Christ left this scene and went back to the glory from which He had come, He began a work which He has been carrying on ever since, and that is His gracious work of intercession on behalf of His people down here in this world. See what we read in our text. He has an unchangeable priesthood. The priests of old did not have an unchangeable priesthood. A man might be a priest for a number of years and intercede with God in behalf of the people, and then when he died somebody else had to take his place; but because our Lord Jesus has an unchangeable priesthood, "He is able also to save them to the uttermost that come unto God by him, seeing he ever liveth to make intercession for them."

The salvation referred to here is not salvation from judgment. It is not salvation from hell, but it is salvation from the power of sin and from the difficulties of the way. What the text tells us is this: That the same Saviour who died for our sins on the cross, who gave Himself there a ransom for our souls, now lives in heaven, and there He is engaged in His gracious work of intercession, that He might save us practically day by day as we go on through this scene.

He wills that I should holy be;
Who can withstand His will?
The counsel of His grace in me
He surely shall fulfill.

He has saved me to make me holy, to conform me to His own likeness; and in order that this blessed work may be wrought out in me, He is interceding with God the Father on my behalf.

"He is able also to save them to the uttermost that come unto God by him, seeing he ever liveth to make intercession for them." That expression, "to the uttermost" really means "forevermore." He is able to save them forevermore. He is able to take us through every difficulty, through every trial, through every perplexity, through every danger. He is able to give us the strength we need in order to surmount all these things and to live triumphant, victorious Christian lives. He is everything that we are not naturally but which we ought to be, and He is all this in order that He may conform us to Himself and make us as He is.

"Such an high priest became us (was suited to us), who is holy, harmless, undefiled, separate from sinners, and made higher than the heavens." We in ourselves are unholy instead of holy; we are harmful instead of harmless. We have often been defiled and alas, alas, we have mingled with the godless and have learned their ways and become like them. But He is the very opposite to all this, and all that He is He is for us. It is His will to make us partners of His holiness, and to enable us to live in this world blameless and holy, and to walk before Him, separate from everything that would defile us, everything that would hinder the manifestation of Christ in our lives. We love that little chorus that Gipsy Smith has so popularized wherever he has gone:

> Let the beauty of Jesus be seen in me,
>   All His wonderful passion and purity.
> O, thou Spirit divine,
>   All my nature refine,
> Till the beauty of Jesus is seen in me.

It is not that there is any change in our old corrupt nature, but the word *nature,* of course, is used by the poet to designate our innermost being, our true character; and oh, how our risen, glorified Lord delights to so work in His people as to transform their lives and establish them by grace.

Have you ever known any of these transformed people? I have known thousands of them. I could tell of scores of Christians with whom I am well acquainted, men and women who once walked with the world but craved what the world never gave—men and women who were once subject to many sins and to the power of Satan. Many of them struggled for years against these things, and tried to free themselves, but they found themselves only in deeper trouble and distress. And then one day they heard the grand and glorious gospel of the grace of God. They learned that Christ died for their sins, was buried, and rose again, and that God has set Him forth a Prince and a Saviour, and that all who put their trust in Him have forgiveness of sins; and they came to Him just as they were and trusted Him. They believed in Him as their own Saviour, and the moment they looked to Him, a great change took place. Perhaps they were not aware of it all at once, but they knew something had happened— there was a change within. They were born again, regenerated by the Word and the Spirit of God, and then there was a change manifested without. The old habits, the old ways fell off like the dead leaves fall from the trees when the sap begins to rise in the springtime and flows out into the limbs. The new life drove out the old desires.

Long years ago a great Scotch minister, Dr. Chalmers, preached a sermon that has been considered a classic in pulpit oratory ever since—"The Expulsive Power of a New Affection." Having learned to love Christ, old things pass away and all things become new. I have watched many of these people and have seen them grow and develop day after day and week after week and month after month, and today you would hardly know them.

I remember so well when I was over in Scotland a few years ago. We were holding the meetings in the Tent Hall and thousands of people were coming to hear the Word. So often before the preaching had actually begun there would be a kind of a testimony meeting, and Jock Troup would call on various ones for a testimony. There were two old ladies—they call them grannies over there— that I especially liked to hear. Jock would say, "Granny So-and-So, step up and give us a testimony," and this dear old woman with such a sweet, kind face would get up and tell how the Lord had saved her. I would think, Oh my, there must be years of holy living back of all that. And then the other one would be called on, and it would have just the same effect; and then Jock would lean over and whisper to me, "When they came here just a few years back, they were just poor, hopeless drunkards, lost to everything good and decent and respectable. They entered in rags and were so drunk that we thought they couldn't under- stand, but they were pointed to Christ and were saved; they were transformed from poor old drunken derelicts into glorious saints of the Lord, and they have been kept by Him, growing more and more like Jesus all the time."

That is the effect of His intercessory work. He is up there talking to the Father on our behalf. If you want to know what He says, read the seventeenth chapter of John, for it is just a sample of our Lord's intercession as our great High Priest. He prays for His own. He prays that they may be sanctified by the Truth. He prays that they may be kept from the evil that is in the world, that they may manifest Him down here in this scene. And when we draw from Him, as we recognize Him as our High Priest and Intercessor, as we come to Him we receive the power that we need to live to His glory in this world.

Turn back to Hebrews, chapter 4, verse 14, and read on to the end of the chapter:

> Seeing then that we have a great high priest, that is passed into the heavens, Jesus the Son of God, let us hold fast our profession. For we have not an high priest which cannot be touched with the feeling of our infirmities; but was in all points tempted like as we are, yet without sin. Let us therefore come boldly unto the throne of grace, that we may obtain mercy, and find grace to help in time of need.

There, you see, you have the blessed Lord seated at the Father's right hand, our High Priest, our Intercessor, and we are invited to come to Him and to come with boldness, not with hesitancy, not feeling that perhaps we won't be welcome, but to come readily, gladly, boldly, and bring to Him the story of our need, our trials, our disappointments; and we receive as we thus come to Him mercy, mercy because of failure and sin, that we may be forgiven. We all need His mercy, and we need grace to help in time of need. That is, it is not the grace by which we are saved from our sins, from the judgment due to sin, but it is grace ministered to us to empower us to resist temptation, and thus to live to His glory.

He is there as our great High Priest and Intercessor, as our Forerunner, in order that He may lead us in our worship as we come into the very presence of God. In Hebrews, chapter 10, verses 19 through 22, we read:

> Having therefore, brethren, boldness to enter into the holiest by the blood of Jesus, by a new and living way, which he hath

consecrated for us, through the veil, that is to say, his flesh; and having an high priest over the house of God; let us draw near with a true heart in full assurance of faith, having our hearts sprinkled from an evil conscience, and our bodies washed with pure water.

Because He is there in the presence of God, in the holiest of all, and has made full atonement for sin, we are now invited to enter within the veil. The veil has been rent; there is nothing to separate, and we can come direct to God. We do not need a mediator apart from Christ Himself. We do not need to call upon anyone else—saint or angel. We do not need to look to anyone but our blessed, risen, glorified Lord, and in His name we come into the presence of the Father and we bring to Him the adoring expression of our grateful hearts. We worship Him and bring to Him our petitions, assured that He will undertake for us.

Then if we fail, when we are actually conscious of sin, He is there interceding on our behalf. We read in First John, chapter 2 and verse 1, R. V., "My little children, these things write I unto you that ye may not sin." That is the ideal for the Christian, but immediately he adds, realizing our weakness:

> And if any man sin, we have an Advocate with the Father, Jesus Christ the righteous: and he is the propitiation for our sins; and not for ours only, but also for the whole world.

My dear young brother or sister, you who have recently come to Christ, sometimes you get discouraged when you try and fail, when temptation comes and you forget to look to the Lord for help and you go down. Well, do not let the devil keep you down. Say to him: "Rejoice not against me, O mine enemy: when I fall, I shall arise; when I sit in darkness, the LORD shall be a light unto me." You may look right up into heaven and you may see there by faith our Advocate in the presence of the Father to intercede for you. Satan is there to accuse, but our Advocate is there to meet every accusation and His precious blood is the answer to every failure. He says, "I took that sin into account when I died at Calvary," so that no sin that you have ever committed has been unatoned for. But now, strengthened and encouraged to know that you are not cast out because of your failure, you come to Him for help in the future, even as you bow before God and in contrition confess your sin, and then you may say, "He is faithful and just to forgive us our sins, and to cleanse us from all unrighteousness." Well, so much then for the intercession of our blessed Lord at God's right hand.

Now another aspect of intercession is the intercession of the Holy Spirit. The Lord Jesus is called our Advocate, as we noticed in that last scripture. The Spirit is called the Comforter. Everybody may not be aware of the fact that in the Greek language from which our New Testament is translated these two words are exactly the same. The Greek word *parakletos* is translated *Advocate* in one place and *Comforter* in another. It means one who comes to your side to help, to help in the hour of need. You have the Lord Jesus as your Intercessor, also as Advocate and Comforter in heaven, and the Holy Spirit as Advocate and Comforter here on earth. We read in Romans, chapter 8, verse 26:

> Likewise the Spirit also helpeth our infirmities: for we know not what we should pray for as we ought: but the Spirit itself maketh intercession for us with groanings which cannot be uttered.

Do you know what the Apostle means? You may often be in circumstances where you really do not know what to say when you kneel before God in prayer. Terrific pressure is being brought against your soul and you are not quite sure what the will of God is. You bow before Him and do not know what to say. At that very time the

Holy Spirit who dwells within you makes intercession. He knows what is right—He knows the will of God for you, and He makes intercession within you with groanings that cannot be uttered. And we are told in the next verse,

> He that searcheth the hearts knoweth what is the mind of the Spirit, because he maketh intercession for the saints according to the will of God (Rom. 8:27).

And so, my brother, when you do not know what to pray for or how to pray, you get down before God and if you cannot do anything else, remain there on your knees in silence and let the Holy Spirit of God who dwells within you voice your petitions. Let Him make intercession and be assured that God will answer.

So many of our young men today are facing problems that perplex them. Here is a young man, we will say, who has an aged mother dependent upon him and yet he is subject to his country's call. He might feel like praying that he might be allowed to remain at home and care for his mother. On the other hand, he is a patriotic American. He says, "I ought not to be willing to stay at home and let other fellows go out there and fight for me," and so he does not know just how to pray. He can kneel before God and say, "Lord, I do not know what to pray for in this situation, but oh, wilt Thou not have Thine own way?" As he puts it up to the Lord, the Holy Spirit makes intercession according to the will of God, and whichever way the answer comes, that young man can say, "I am satisfied that it is the will of God, and I will accept His will."

So often other questions arise. Perhaps a loved one is very, very ill, suffering terribly from some malignant disease. Our natural thought is, "O Lord, won't you heal this dear one?" and yet on the other hand the thought comes that perhaps after all it might be God's holy will to take this loved one home to be with Himself. You do not know how to pray. You do not know what to ask. Very well, bow before God and say, "Lord, here is the case." Spread it out before Him and say, "Now, Lord, not my will but Thine be done." Let the Holy Spirit take the case to God. He will make intercession according to the perfect will of God with groanings that cannot be uttered. You won't hear a sound, but God will hear, and the answer will be in accordance with his own blessed will.

And then there is a third aspect of intercession that we must not pass over, and that is the intercession of believers. The first Epistle to Timothy, chapter 2, verses 1 through 6:

> I exhort therefore, that, first of all, supplications, prayers, intercessions, and giving of thanks, be made for all men; for kings, and for all that are in authority; that we may lead a quiet and peaceable life in all godliness and honesty. For this is good and acceptable in the sight of God our Saviour; who will" (that is, He desires), "who will have all men to be saved, and to come unto the knowledge of the truth. For there is one God, and one mediator between God and men, the man Christ Jesus; who gave himself a ransom for all, to be testified in due time.

Now here the Spirit of God through the apostle is putting upon us the responsibility of intercession, and what a remarkable privilege this is! Here is a Christian, perhaps poor as to this world's goods, hardly known outside the block in which she lives, perhaps scarcely known outside the little apartment in which she dwells; but this Christian has the wonderful privilege of access to the throne of God, and she can go into her little room alone, kneel there before God, and she can start things going from that room which will affect individuals, families, communities, churches, and nations for good. Is not that an amazing thing?

Let me give you an instance. On one of the first occasions that Mr. Moody went to Great Britain, the very first time he went, in fact, he was disappointed to find that the man who invited him over there had died while he was on the way, and nobody seemed to be on hand to welcome him. Finally, a certain pastor got in touch with him and said, "Mr. Moody, will you preach for us?" He agreed to do so and was to preach on Sunday morning and Sunday night, and I think to continue for several nights. A young woman who listened to him that Sunday morning hurried home and said to an invalid sister, "Who do you think preached in our church this morning?" The sister said, "I don't know."

"Dwight L. Moody," came the reply.

"Dwight L. Moody of Chicago—the great Sunday school worker?" That is the way he was known then.

"Yes," she said, "and sister, right here in this room we have been praying for months that God would send D. L. Moody from Chicago to our church!" And God had brought him all the way across the sea and had so ordered his providential arrangements that out of all the churches in England, that was the only one to which he was invited that Sunday. Oh, the power of intercessory prayer, when the one who prays is in touch with God!

Consider the present world crisis. Oh, if Christians were only stirred to pray as they should, I have no hesitation in saying that victory would come for righteousness in a very, very short time indeed, and every foe of liberty and of Christianity would be destroyed. "Pray," says the Lord Jesus, "to thy Father which is in secret; and thy Father which seeth in secret shall reward thee openly." We should intercede on behalf of others, on behalf of those in high places, on behalf of all men everywhere, on behalf of the work of God, on behalf of our nation, on behalf of Israel in their present agony, on behalf of the troubled nations everywhere. It is our privilege to intercede with God, coming to Him in the name of our great High Priest, the Lord

Jesus Christ, the one Mediator between God and men. We need no other. We do not need to go to St. Peter, or St. Paul, or St. Jude, or to Michael the archangel, or to any of the rest of them, but we go to God our Father in the name of the Lord Jesus Christ, our Mediator and Advocate, directed and guided by the Holy Spirit who dwells within us.

# VII

# RESURRECTION

He preached unto them Jesus, and the resurrection . . . And
the times of this ignorance God winked at; but now commandeth
all men everywhere to repent: because he hath appointed a day,
in the which he will judge the world in righteousness by that
man whom he hath ordained; whereof he hath given assurance
unto all men, in that he hath raised him from the dead (Acts
17:18, 30, 31).

APART from the great fact of the resurrection of our
Lord Jesus Christ from the dead we would have no
gospel to preach. By "resurrection" we do not mean
that our Lord's spirit continued to live after His body died,
but that He was actually raised from the dead by the glory
of the Father, and came forth from the tomb in the very
same body that had been impaled on Calvary's cross. In
that body, now glorified, He sits at God's right hand, and
in that same body He is coming again as the Judge of both
living and dead—the saved and the lost. This is what is
emphasized for us in the seventeenth chapter of the Acts
of the Apostles.

The entire passage, beginning with verse 16, is of tremendous interest, but I have no thought of attempting to
explain it all, though I hope you will read it carefully at
your leisure, if you are not thoroughly familiar with it,
for it is undoubtedly one of the finest examples of a preacher's eloquence that we have anywhere in the Bible.

Paul appears here at his best, from the human standpoint, but he also speaks as a divinely inspired servant
of Christ. Of Apollos we read elsewhere that he was an
eloquent man and mighty in the Scriptures, and it is very
evident from this sample sermon that Paul was a man of
the same stamp; although on the other hand he did not

particularly cultivate what was simply rhetorical, lest the Cross of Christ should be made of none effect.

But it was quite in keeping with his principle of being "made all things to all men," that, when he stood on Mars' Hill, the very center of culture of the Greek world, he should meet those

### Proud Attic Philosophers

on their own ground. So far as culture was concerned, he was every whit their equal, combining a thorough acquaintance with their literature, history and customs, with a deep knowledge of the Word of God to which they were strangers. Thus he gave them that day a new and arresting message such as they had never heard before, and possibly many were destined never to hear again.

Notice some of the circumstances. Paul was waiting in Athens for several of his fellow servants, who had returned to Thessalonica to find out how the newborn Christians there were getting along. As he wandered about the city, his spirit was deeply stirred, for he saw everywhere the evidences of idolatry. They worshipped everything in Athens, in fact an ancient philosopher once said, "In Athens it is easier to find a god than a man." There were images on every street corner, over every doorway, in every courtyard, found in every store, and every dwelling house. Turn where you would, you were confronted by these

### Signs of Pagan Darkness

and Paul, as he walked those streets, knew that the things the Gentiles sacrificed were sacrificed to demons and not to God; he knew that he was probably the only man in that city who had a knowledge of the true and living God and of His Son, the Lord Jesus Christ; and yet for the time being he saw no opportunity to give his message in a public way.

A Jewish synagogue, however, attracted his attention, and

entering it, he claimed his right as a recognized teacher to speak, and there he presented the gospel, disputing with the adherents of Judaism, and with proselytes who were doubtless weary of the unsatisfactory character of idolatrous rites and ceremonies, and had sought out this place of instruction in the law of Moses.

In the market place also he addressed himself to individuals, and sometimes little groups would gather about him to whom he proclaimed the wondrous story of God's grace in Christ Jesus to a lost world. Little by little he drew the attention of the people, who were always interested in that which seemed new and strange. So we need not be surprised that at last certain philosophers of the Epicureans and the Stoics became interested in him and his teaching.

### The Epicureans

were those who said that man's supreme good is found in trying to please himself, that there is no use denying one's-self; make the best of life by getting all the pleasure out of it you can, for you are going to be dead a long time. We can hear the echo of this in the philosophy of so-called self-expression of our day.

The Stoics took the opposite view of life. They said: we are in the hands of a remorseless fate; we had nothing to say about coming into the world, and there is no telling what will happen when we leave it. Just grit your teeth, don't show the white feather, make up your mind that "what cannot be cured must be endured." Stoicism has come down through the ages as the synonym for patient endurance.

Some of these philosophers asked, "What will this babbler say?" To them he seemed to be setting forth new gods. New gods in Athens! They had searched the world to find all of them. They had shrines for the gods of

Babylon, Phoenicia, Greece, Egypt, and Rome. They worshipped them all, and yet this man seemed to know something about some new ones, because Paul preached "Jesus and the resurrection." They thought that Anastasis (resurrection) was another god. They had the god of peace, the god of victory, the god of justice, the god of love—all these different deified human attributes; and now they thought, "This man seems to have two new gods, one called Jesus and the other, Resurrection. We would like to hear more about them." And they took him up to Mars' Hill, or the Areopagus. This overlooked Athens, and was where the philosophers met for discussion. So they invited Paul to come up there and expound his new doctrines. Led by them, he wended his way to the meeting-place above, and at once began to proclaim the message that he had been yearning to give them for so long.

He took his text from an inscription he had seen on one of their altars, and said, as it were, "I see you are a very religious people. You seem to worship every god known to the Greeks and all other nations, and as I walked about I noticed an altar with the inscription,

*'To the Unknown God!'*"

(Just such an altar has been unearthed recently.) It was evident that these Athenians feared lest they might be neglecting some god whose name had not been communicated to them, and so they set up the altar that had attracted Paul's attention.

What a splendid text it made! And so Paul said, "Whom therefore ye ignorantly worship, him declare I unto you." In other words, "I am here to tell you who the unknown God is." How can anyone make known the unknown? God has made Himself known in the person of His blessed Son, the Lord Jesus Christ. Paul was there, indeed, to present Jesus and the resurrection, and let me say that no man preaches the gospel unless he does preach Jesus and the resurrection.

There is no gospel for guilty sinners apart from Christ, for the gospel is God's message about His blessed Son. The gospel is not good advice to be obeyed; *it is good news to be believed*. And that good news concerns the Lord Jesus Christ who came from the glory that He had with the Father from all eternity down to the sorrow and anguish of the cross of Calvary where He bared His breast that the sword of divine justice might be sheathed in His heart. He took our place and endured what we deserved. But that alone would not be the gospel; there is something more needed. Paul preached

### Jesus, AND—

And what? "*And* the resurrection." Every sermon that he ever preached was an Easter sermon; every sermon that the early apostles preached was an Easter sermon, for wherever they went they preached that Christ *died* for our sins according to the Scriptures: and that He was *buried*, and that He *rose again* the third day according to the Scriptures. The essence of their message was that He "was delivered for our offences, and was raised again for our justification" (Romans 4:25).

So Paul preached Jesus and the resurrection, and we today proclaim the same, and we tell you in His Name, "That if thou shalt confess with thy mouth the Lord Jesus, and shalt believe in thine heart that God hath raised him from the dead, thou shalt be saved. For with the heart man believeth unto righteousness; and with the mouth confession is made unto salvation" (Romans 10:9, 10).

### The Creator and the Created

Notice how Paul prepared the ground for his message. First of all, they were reminded that the Creator must be greater than that which is created, and Paul directed their attention to the visible universe. It was very evident that the God who made all things could not be confined in one of their temples He says, "God that made the world and all things therein, seeing that he is Lord of heaven and earth, dwelleth not in temples made with hands; neither is worshipped with men's hands, as though he needed any thing, seeing he giveth to all life, and breath, and all things." He is not the God of one nation, but of all nations, and we are really one people, for He "hath made of one blood all nations of men for to dwell on all the face of the earth, and hath determined the times before appointed, and the bounds of their habitation." He has put upon men the responsibility to know Him, for He is not far from any one of us.

There is no man anywhere who will dare say in the day of judgment, "I wanted to find God and could not," for

> Closer is He than breathing,
> Nearer than hands and feet.

He is so close that if men will feel after Him, will stretch up empty hands towards Him, they will find His great strong hands reaching down to lay hold of them. God will never permit it to be said that any man honestly sought the way of life and failed to find it, that any man really wanted to be saved, and cried to God unheard.

This answers a question that troubles a good many people. I am often asked,

### "What About the Heathen

that have never heard the gospel? Are they going to be damned because they have never heard?" No matter where a heathen man may be today, if he wants to know God and honestly reaches out after Him, God will make Himself responsible to give that man light enough to be saved, for He is not far from any one of us. God has commanded men "that they should seek the Lord, if haply they might feel after him, and find him."

This is the only place in the New Testament where we get the word *feel*. I have often urged people to trust the Lord Jesus, and have told them how He died for them, bore their sins on the cross, and that if they will believe on Him, He has given His own Word that "whosoever believeth in him should not perish, but have everlasting life." And then they say, "Well, I do *believe,* but I don't *feel* any different." That has nothing to do with it. The word *feel* is not a Christian word at all. The only place it occurs in the New Testament is here where Paul is speaking of the heathen. But you have an open Bible; you do not need to feel after God. What you need to do is to *believe* the testimony that He has given, and then you will be saved. "Believe on the Lord Jesus Christ, and thou shalt be saved, and thy house" (Acts 16:31). This is the word of the living God given through His servants of old.

### *"Feel" and "Feeling"*

I said that the word *feel* is found only once in the New Testament, but the word *feeling* is found twice: once in Ephesians 4:19, where it speaks of certain Gentiles, and says, "Who being past feeling have given themselves over unto lasciviousness, to work all uncleanness with greediness"; and again in Hebrews 4:15, "For we have not an high priest which cannot be touched with the feeling of our infirmities." Apart from these three instances we do not find the words *feeling* or *feel* used in the New Testament. The moment you believe in the Lord Jesus, the moment you trust in Him you pass out of death into life, out of condemnation into justification before the throne of God.

In John 5:24, Jesus says, "Verily, verily, I say unto you,

He that heareth my word, and believeth him that sent me, hath everlasting life, and shall not come into condemnation; but is passed from death unto life." Notice the

### FIVE DIVISIONS OF JOHN 5:24

1. "HE THAT HEARETH MY WORD." Face this; be honest with your own heart. Have you heard the Word of the Son of God? Have you heard Him speaking to you through this blessed Book?

2. "AND BELIEVETH HIM THAT SENT ME." Do you in your heart believe that God sent the Lord Jesus Christ to be the sinner's Saviour, to die for you on the cross, to rise from the dead for your justification?

3. "HATH EVERLASTING LIFE." When do you get it? When you die? No, you get it *now,* from the moment you believe, from the moment you hear the Word of the Son of God, and receive and confess Him as the One whom the Father sent into the world to be the sinner's Saviour. The trouble today is that people are stumbling over its very simplicity.

I heard of a man who wanted to be saved, and he was told to do penance for sin by putting hard dried peas in his shoes and walking on them so many hours a day. This poor man did this and limped around the streets, trying to make atonement. It would have done him just as much good if he had boiled the peas first.

But people are willing to do all kinds of hard things. They are like Naaman who, when the prophet commanded, "Go and wash in Jordan seven times," said, "That is too easy a way." But he had a wise old servant who suggested, "If the prophet had bid thee do some *great* thing, wouldest thou not have done it?" Why, of course he would. "How much rather then, when he saith to thee, Wash, and be clean?" If you had to give a great deal of money, say a great many prayers, make long pilgrimages, do vast numbers of charitable deeds in order to get life eternal, how many of you would be willing to do these things? How much more when He saith to thee, *"Believe and live!"*

4. "SHALL NOT COME INTO CONDEMNATION." Think of it! The Roman Catholic Version reads, "Amen, amen, I say unto you, whoso hears my word and believes him that sent me, has eternal life and comes not into judgment, but is passed out of death into life." Is that not good news? Not a word about purgatory, not a word about confession to a priest, not a word about sacramental observances, not a word about penance; but here and now, the moment you put your trust in the Lord Jesus Christ, your sins are gone and you will never come into judgment, but you have everlasting life. It is all for you. That is the gospel which Paul preached. And notice the next point:

5. "IS PASSED FROM DEATH UNTO LIFE." It is a settled, complete salvation, giving a new standing before God to the believing sinner. Observe the threefold link with resurrection:

### 1. *Resurrection and Repentance*

But what if men do not accept it? Then there is the judgment. He says that God has been very gracious with the heathen: "The times of this ignorance God winked at; but now commandeth all men everywhere to *repent*." Repent means to change your mind completely, to have a new attitude. You had an idea that you could save yourself by your good works, but you change your mind and now admit that you cannot do a thing to save yourself, but that Christ must do it all. That is repentance—a change of attitude toward God. Instead of trying to do anything to save yourself, let the Lord Jesus do it all.

God "commandeth all men everywhere to repent: because he hath appointed a day, in the which he will judge the world in righteousness by that man whom he hath ordained." God is going to judge the world in righteousness, but your case can be settled out of court, and settled today, so that you need never think of coming into judgment. But if you reject Christ, some day you must give account before His judgment throne.

## 2. Resurrection and Assurance

"Whereof he hath given *assurance* unto all men, in that he hath raised him from the dead." The resurrection of the body of our Lord Jesus Christ is the ground of our assurance that we shall live again in our resurrected bodies. He says, "Because I live, ye shall live also." We are told that "As in Adam all die, even so in Christ shall all be made alive." This does not mean that all men will be saved, but that the bodies of all men will be raised from the dead. Thus God has given assurance to all men of a life after death in that He raised the body of Christ from the grave. In the second place He has given assurance unto all men that the sin question is settled in the death of Christ, by raising His body from the dead.

Here is an innocent man who has gone to prison for the crime of another. He knew the other man was guilty, but he knew, too, that in order to prove his own innocence he would have to expose his friend; and so he hears the sentence of the judge, sending him to prison for one year. What must be the feeling of the other man outside? He says, "I have sent that man there; I deserved to go, but he is there in my place." Perhaps he goes to see him and the man says, "I took your place voluntarily, and I am quite content; you let me endure it." The other roams the streets and says, "I wonder how long he will be content to remain there; I wonder how long before he tells the whole story." But by and by a year has passed, and walking down the street one day, he sees the one who went to prison for him. He rushes up and says, "What does this mean?"

"It means," is the reply, "that you have nothing to fear now. The sentence has all been endured."

So our blessed Lord bore on the Tree the sentence for us, and now we who were once guilty sinners are free. "Christ being raised from the dead dieth no more." The resurrection is the proof that the sin question has been settled, that God is satisfied. "He hath given assurance unto all men, in that he hath raised him from the dead."

### 3. *Resurrection and Reckoning*

In the third place we have assurance in the resurrection of Jesus Christ that some day all men are going to give account to Him. This will be when He sits upon the great white throne. Think of giving account of your sins to Him after all He has done to save you from them!

Notice the threefold response that Paul's message had that day. "When they heard of the resurrection of the dead, some mocked: and others said, We will hear thee again of this matter. . . . Howbeit certain men clave unto him, and believed." I wonder if there are not people manifesting these three different attitudes toward the message today!

Some mock, some ridicule, some say, "Oh, we cannot believe this message about Jesus and the resurrection; we cannot accept it. We do not see how He could die for sinners and rise again, and how men can be saved through believing on Him." God pity you if you are turning this message down. Some day He will turn you down, for He says in His Word, "Because I have called, and ye refused; I have stretched out my hand, and no man regarded; but ye have set at nought all my counsel, and would none of my reproof: I also will laugh at your calamity; I will mock when your fear cometh" (Proverbs 1:24-26). God grant that you may not at last be exposed to such a doom. Do not turn it down, do not go away with a cold, careless sneer and say, "It is nothing to me."

The second class said, "We will hear thee again of this matter." They are the procrastinators. You may not be mocking; possibly you would not sneer at the gospel message; you fully intend to be saved some day, but you are saying, "I will hear you again; I am not ready to close with Christ today. There is so much to occupy my heart and mind these days; some other time. Let me alone for the present. Sometime I will give attention to these things." Remember the old saying, "Procrastination is the thief of time." There is a Spanish proverb which says, "The road of by and by leads to the town of never." How many have taken that road, have said, "By and by, some other day," and have gone on and on, until at last they have reached the other world, hopelessly lost, and that forever!

The third class, "Howbeit certain men clave unto him, and believed." What a blessed testimony! God has recorded the names of two of them, one man and one woman, Dionysius and Damaris, who accepted the message proclaimed that day.

Men have an idea that what sinners need is more culture, more refinement; but if polite culture could have saved the world, Greece would have been saved long ago. *But Greece went all to pieces in spite of its culture.* It was the gospel of the grace of God that saved the ancient world from ruin. And it is the gospel of the Lord Jesus Christ that saves men today. I bring before you these two examples, Dionysius and Damaris, and I beg you to follow them as they followed Christ; believe the message, and go on rejoicing in Him, who was raised from the dead, never to die again. Hear what He says in Revelation 1:18—"I am he that liveth, and was dead; and, behold, I am alive for evermore."

# VIII

# EXPECTATION

IN the eighth chapter of the Epistle to the Romans, reading from verse 18, we have these words:

> For I reckon that the sufferings of this present time are not worthy to be compared with the glory which shall be revealed in us. For the earnest expectation of the creation waiteth for the manifestation of the sons of God. For the creation was made subject to vanity, not willingly, but by reason of him who hath subjected the same in hope, because the creation itself also shall be delivered from the bondage of corruption into the glorious liberty of the children of God. For we know that the whole creation groaneth and travaileth in pain together until now. And not only they, but ourselves also, which have the firstfruits of the Spirit, even we ourselves groan within ourselves, waiting for the adoption, to wit, the redemption of our body.

Then if you will also turn to Philippians, chapter 1, verses 20 and 21:

> According to my earnest expectation and my hope, that in nothing I shall be ashamed, but that with all boldness, as always, so now also Christ shall be magnified in my body, whether it be by life, or by death. For to me to live is Christ, and to die is gain.

The Christian has a wonderful expectation. Our Lord Jesus Christ while He was here on earth had a great deal to say about His second coming. I have never been able to understand why some persons who profess to be Christians (and I would not dare doubt in some instances but that they are really such) seem to have no interest whatever in the truth of the return of our blessed Saviour. I have often heard people say, "I am not interested in the second coming of Christ. The only thing that concerns me is to be ready when He comes."

Of course it is very important that we should be ready when He comes, but to say, "The only thing that concerns me is to be ready for that event," seems to me to be the quintessence of selfishness. Am I only concerned about my personal readiness? Do I not have a deep, warm expectation in my soul, looking forward to that glorious day when the Saviour shall return? Am I not longing to see Him?

He has said that He is coming back, and He told us to watch and to wait for His coming, to be like men that wait for their Lord when He will return from the wedding. And surely if we have learned to love Him, if we know Him as the One who died for us and washed away our sins in His precious blood, we certainly ought to be looking eagerly for His return.

Some people think of the second coming of the Lord as though it were a dreadful event, an event from which we might well shrink, because they confound the second coming of Christ for His people with the day of judgment for a godless world; but these are two very distinct events. When He said, "If I go and prepare a place for you, I will come again, and receive you unto myself; that where I am, there ye may be also," He was not referring to the final day of judgment. He was speaking of the time when He will come back and raise the dead and change the living, those of His own redeemed people, and take them up to be with Him in the Father's house. Surely there is nothing to dread about that. It is no fearful portent, the thought of the Lord's coming.

On one occasion I was asked in a certain Canadian city to give an address to the ministerial union on the second coming of the Lord Jesus, and so I went down with a heart and mind full of the subject, and found nearly seventy of the city's preachers gathered together. It was my privilege to talk to them for about forty minutes on what I believe the Word of God teaches concerning this great expectation of the Church. When I had finished, the moderator of the meeting, who was a Presbyterian minister, rose and said, "My friends, I want to give my personal testimony concerning this subject. I was a minister for a great many years before I ever took the time to study what the Bible has to say about the second coming of the Lord, but some years back I became deeply interested and I searched the Scriptures for all references to the subject. You know, as that truth opened up to me, I got a new Bible. It just seemed as though my Bible was entirely different. So many things were plain that had been dark before." Then he said, "Now I would like to have you tell us how this subject appeals to you."

There happened to be present a very venerable old gentleman, an Anglican clergyman, who had received a great many honors because of his scholarship and ability. He had written a great many books and I had read all of them, so I was quite interested when he was pointed out to me. The moderator knew he was in the audience that day and because he seemed in a certain sense to be the dean of them all, he turned to him and said, "Doctor, wouldn't you like to speak to us on the subject?" The dear old gentleman stood up and in that fine, cultured way that is so characteristic of Anglican clergymen, said something like this: "Well, my dear brother, I am really sorry that you referred to me at all, because I never like to take issue with a visiting speaker. I would far rather have just said to our brother at the close, 'Thank you,' and left it at that; but since you put me on the spot, it is necessary for me to express myself, and I regret to have to say that I do not find myself at all in agreement with the speaker who has addressed us today. Of course, I think there is something in the Bible about the second coming of the Lord, but just what it is I do not know and I do not think anyone else does. In fact, with apologies to our speaker, I do not think he does. I have listened carefully to what he has presented and I have been thinking that if his presentation of the subject is the correct one, it must be an awful thing to believe, as he says he believes, that Christ may come back at any moment. Why, if one believed that, it would unnerve him completely. Suppose I were out making pastoral calls and the awful thought came to me that Christ might come today! I would not be able to continue my work, but would want to get back to my study and read the prayer book and try to get ready for that awful event."

Well, you know it was a little difficult for me. I was much younger than he and I did not want to be discourteous, but I said to him, "Doctor, I hope that you do not mean us to infer that one could have been a member of the great church to which you belong and have taken all the ecclesiastical and academical honors that you have and yet never have been washed from his sins in the precious blood of Christ! For Doctor, if you have been saved through what the Lord Jesus did when He was here the first time, whether you realize it or not, you will be ready when He comes the second time." Because it is not our understanding of the doctrines of our Lord's return that makes us ready to meet Him, or our growth in holiness, but the fact that Another has, in the blessed will of God, shed His blood and died for us, cleansing us from all sin.

To me the expectation of the Lord's imminent return is one of the most precious hopes that I have. I think this is what the apostle meant when he said, 'According to my earnest expectation and my hope.' He was looking for the coming of the Saviour, and he said, "I do not want to be ashamed. I want to be found, while I am watching for him, laboring always for His glory, endeavoring to bring others to Him, and seeking to manifest Christ in my daily life so that I can always say, 'For to me to live is Christ, and to die is gain.'"

This poor world needs the coming Saviour. Suppose our Lord had come ten years ago. Then the world would never have known the dire conflict that is prevailing at the present time. Why do we see the nations engaged in bloody conflict one with the other? It is because when the Prince of Peace came here to dwell amongst men in lowly grace He was not recognized. He was rejected. He came to bring peace but men said, "We will not have this man to reign over us"; and so, according to Hosea He said, "I will go and return to my place, till they acknowledge their offence, and seek my face: in their affliction they will seek me early." He has gone back to the Father's right hand and is there preparing a place for His redeemed. Some day He is coming again and His coming is going to mean the rapture of His Church and our presentation before the Father in fulness of joy.

That is one aspect of it, but the other aspect is this: He is coming back to this poor world and He is going to reign in righteousness for a thousand wonderful years, and then will be fulfilled the prophecy, "They shall beat their swords into plowshares, and their spears into pruninghooks: nation shall not lift up sword against nation, neither shall they learn war any more" (Micah 4:3). Oh, how the world needs Christ, who is that "blessed and only Potentate, the King of kings, and Lord of lords!"

That is what the apostle is referring to, especially in the eighth chapter of the book of Romans, when he says that "the earnest expectation of the *creation* [rather than simply *creature*] waiteth for the manifestation of the sons of God," for creation's blessing will come with that manifestation. And when will the sons of God be manifested? The sons of God are already in the world at this time, but their manifestation has not come yet. They are in the world but the world knows them not, even as it knew Him not; but we read that when He is manifested, then shall we be manifested. When He reigns, then we will appear with Him in glory! That will be the time when earth's blessing will come, when creation will be liberated from the bondage of the curse.

Look at John's Gospel, chapter 14, the passage we all love and the portion which I think fits in so well at every Christian funeral. I do not know that I have ever been called upon to say a few words at the burial of a saint of God but that I have felt I must read these words: "Ye believe in God, believe also in me." That is, Christ is saying in effect, "I am going away from you, so you won't be able to see me; but you believe in God the Father, though you cannot see Him. Now I want you to believe in me, God the Son, when you cannot see me." And so He has gone back to the Father. We cannot see Him, but we love Him and we love to serve Him, and we wait for His return.

"In my Father's house are many mansions," many resting places, many abodes. It is the same word as the one translated "abode" a little farther down in the chapter: "We will come unto him, and make our abode with him" (verse 23). So He says, "In my Father's house are many abodes, many places of rest." Many of God's dear children know very little of rest here, but they will rest there in the presence of God and His Son when they put on their resurrection bodies.

"If it were not so, I would have told you." There are so many things that the saint of God longs for that perhaps are not based upon positive scripture, but He says, "If this were not a fact, if this hope, this expectation were not

based on truth, I would have told you. I would not want
you to be deluded; I would not want you to be deceived."
When we look forward to resting in His presence, when
we think of heaven as the Father's house, it is not just a
lovely dream, it is not mere imagination. It is a blessed,
precious truth vouched for by our Lord Jesus Himself. He
came from the Father and went to the cross for our redemption. He has gone back to the Father to prepare a
place for us.

I love to think of heaven as a home. Some of us have
not known very much of a home here on earth. It is said
of the one who wrote that most beautiful of all songs about
home, that he was a wanderer all his life. I refer, of
course, to John Howard Payne who wrote, "Home, Sweet
Home." Some of us have not enjoyed much of the com-
forts of home down here on earth, but oh, what a home
He is preparing for us up yonder!

At death the believer goes home, but that is not the final
thing, that is not the fulness of our expectation, for the
Lord Jesus says, "If I go and prepare a place for you, I
will come again, and receive you unto myself; that where
I am, there ye may be also." Dear young Christian, do
get hold of this truth in the early days of your Christian
life. The Lord Jesus says, "I will come again." How can
anybody say he doesn't believe in the second coming of
Christ in view of a promise like that? It is amazing how
people twist those words to try to make them say anything
but what they really say.

Some people tell us that He simply meant that He was
coming to individual souls when they were converted, to
dwell in their hearts. That is not what He is talking about.
He says, "I am going to receive them unto myself, that
where I am there they may be also." There are other folk
who think that when the Lord said those words He was

referring to the descent of the Holy Spirit on the day of Pentecost, that the Holy Spirit, being Jesus' other self, came down to make good this promise. But I think that when people talk like that, they forget that the great bulk of the promises of the second coming in the New Testament were given after the Holy Spirit came at Pentecost. It was after the Holy Spirit fulfilled the Lord's words and came as the Comforter that He moved the hearts of saints to cry, "Even so, come, Lord Jesus," and to look on with eager, glad expectation to His personal return.

Then some people say, "Well, it just means that He is coming in the hour of death. When the believer comes down to death, the Lord will be there to take him home to heaven." And yet, if it is just as true now as it was before the cross that angels transport ransomed souls to heaven, it is a very different thing from the personal coming of Christ. The beggar Lazarus died and was carried by angels to Abraham's bosom, and I suppose that angels take the saints now into the presence of the Lord. "Are they not all ministering spirits, sent forth to minister for them who shall be heirs of salvation?" (Hebrews 1:14). But Jesus speaks of a personal coming. That is not death; it is the destruction of death for the believer.

Then there are some people who confound the Lord's return with the judgment day. There is nothing about the judgment here. "If I go and prepare a place for you, I will come again, and receive you unto myself; that where I am, there ye may be also." There is no hint of a judgment day there. It is the returning bridegroom coming for His bride and taking her with Him into the Father's house to share the rest and the glory of that blessed place. The manner of it is described for us in the fourth chapter of the first Epistle to the Thessalonians, a passage with which we are all familiar, unless it be those to whom these things are new and strange. Beginning with verse 13 we read:

> But I would not have you to be ignorant, brethren, concerning them which are asleep, that ye sorrow not, even as others which have no hope. For if we believe that Jesus died and rose again, even so them also which sleep in Jesus will God bring with him. For this we say unto you by the word of the Lord, that we which are alive and remain unto the coming of the Lord shall not prevent (or precede them) which are asleep. For the Lord himself (Notice how distinctly personal that is!) shall descend from heaven with a shout, with the voice of the archangel, and with the trump of God: and the dead in Christ shall rise first.

See the contrast between the Lord's coming and death. Death is not the Saviour's return, but when the Saviour returns, death is destroyed for the believer.

> The dead in Christ shall rise first: then we which are alive and remain shall be caught up together with them in the clouds, to meet the Lord in the air.

You see, there will be the two classes of believers who will have part in the glorious event of the Lord's return. There will be those who are asleep, that is the saints who have died. The bodies of many of them have gone back to the dust from which they came, but they will be raised and those bodies tenanted again by the glorified soul and spirit of the believers. But then there is another group—the believers actually living in this world when Christ returns.

> Then we which are alive and remain shall be caught up together with them in the clouds, to meet the Lord in the air: and so shall we ever be with the Lord (I Thessalonians 4:17).

Would it not be a wonderful thing if we Christians who are living today should be among that number! If, before death claims our bodies, the Saviour should return and we would be caught up together with the resurrected saints in clouds to meet the Lord in the air! Of course, these bodies of ours will have to undergo a great change in order that that may be, but in Philippians 3 we read of that change:

> For our conversation (or citizenship) is in heaven; from whence also we look for the Saviour, the Lord Jesus Christ: who shall change our vile body.

or literally, "transform the body of our humiliation." This body, you see, is called the body of our humiliation. You know how often you are humiliated by your body, don't you? It is such a drag on the spirit at times. Well, when the Saviour comes, He will change the body of our humiliation,

> that it may be fashioned like unto his glorious body, according to the working whereby he is able even to subdue all things unto himself (vv. 20, 21).

We read of this more particularly in the first Epistle to the Corinthians, chapter 15, beginning with verse 51. There the apostle says:

> Behold, I shew you a mystery (I tell you a secret, something nobody knew anything of until it was revealed); We shall not all sleep (that is, we shall not all die), but we shall all be changed (whether living or dead, we shall all be changed), in a moment, in the twinkling of an eye, at the last trump (the trump that ends this dispensation of grace): for the trumpet shall sound, and the dead shall be raised incorruptible, and we shall be changed. For this corruptible must be put on incorruption (that is, the dead, the corrupted bodies of the dead will be raised in incorruption), and this mortal (that is, the living) must be put on immortality.

Those who are now living in mortal bodies will suddenly be given immortal bodies when Jesus comes back again, and in those bodies will live forever.

> So when this corruptible shall have put on incorruption, and this mortal shall have put on immortality, then shall be brought to pass the saying that is written, Death is swallowed up in victory.

No wonder the apostle can exult in triumph:

"O death, where is thy sting? O grave, where is thy victory?" He says:

> The sting of death is sin; and the strength of sin is the law. But thanks be to God, which giveth us the victory through our Lord Jesus Christ.

This, then, is our expectation; this is our hope! And the Lord would have us living day by day in view of the possible fulfillment of the promise of His coming again. When you get up in the morning, cultivate the attitude of soul that leads you to say, "Christ may come today; and if He were to come today, I want Him to find me living for His glory. I want Him to find me walking in obedience to His holy Word." And when you go to sleep at night say, "Christ Jesus may come tonight, and I can rest in perfect peace, knowing that when He comes I shall be caught up to meet Him."

# IX

# MANIFESTATION

I am going to ask your attention to the fifth chapter of the second Epistle to the Corinthians, verses 9 and 10:

> Wherefore we labour, that, whether present or absent, we may be accepted of him. For we must all appear before the judgment seat of Christ; that every one may receive the things done in his body, according to that he hath done, whether it be good or bad.

The second clause might be translated, "We must all be manifested before the judgment seat of Christ," and that is what I ask you to consider: the word "manifestation."

It will be a wonderful day when those who know the Lord and love Him shall appear in His presence, and when He will go back with us over all the path we have come since His grace has saved us. He will point out everything in our lives and service that has been in accordance with His own holy Word, everything that has been the result of the working of the Holy Spirit within us, and for all of that there will be a special reward in that day. He will also manifest all the selfishness, all the carelessness, all the worldliness, the lack of spirituality that has characterized many of us. He will show how we have missed our opportunities; how we could have been more faithful; how we could have been more devoted. But we were indifferent to the call of the Spirit of God, and because of all this we will suffer loss in that day.

I want you to notice several scriptures that bring this thought before us, looking first at verse 9 which we have already read:

*Wherefore we labour, that, whether present or absent, we may be accepted of him.*

"Wherefore we labour," we make it our aim, we are ambitious, we have a laudable ambition, as we are going on in this scene for Christ. And what is that laudable ambition? That whether we remain in the body, or whether we go home to be with the Lord—for that is what is involved in the expression, "whether present or absent"— we will be well-pleasing unto Him.

Do not confound this statement with a very similar expression in Ephesians 1:6, which has an altogether different meaning. There we read, "He," that is, God "hath made us," we who believe, "accepted in the beloved." Now that is true of every Christian. It is true of you who not very long ago were still walking in the world, with the worldlings, had not yet received Christ; but now you have trusted Him. The moment you put your trust in the Lord Jesus, God made you accepted in the Beloved. That is, God received you at that moment according to all the value that He put upon the person and work of His Son. What a wonderful thing that is! Accepted in Him!

What does it mean? It just means this: that the believer is as dear to the heart of the Father as the Lord Jesus is; that God thinks as much of you who have trusted Christ as He does of His own blessed Son. That may seem hard to believe; in fact, I could not believe it if I did not find it in my Bible, but I do find it there. In John 17, I hear the Lord Jesus praying to the Father and He uses this language: "That the world may know that thou hast sent me, and hast loved them, as thou hast loved me" (v. 23). Those are the Saviour's own words. He says of every believer, of every child of God through faith in His name, of everyone of them, no matter what their experience may have been: "Thou hast loved them, as thou hast loved me."

There is another verse in the first Epistle of John that is very striking. It says there, "As he is," that is, as Christ is, "so are we in this world" (4:17). I remember years ago when I just could not take that in. I would read those words, "As he is, so are we in this world," and I would say to myself, "Oh no, not I! I am not as holy, I am not as righteous as He is. I am not as loving, I am not as compassionate, I am not as much concerned about lost sinners as He is." I could not say that I am as He is right down here in this world. I felt as though I could have understood it better if it had said, "As he is, so *shall* we be when we leave this world," for I confidently hoped to become some day exactly like Him; but to say, "As he is, so *are* we in this world," that was altogether too much for me in those days. I felt that I could have understood if He had said, "As he is, so *ought* we to be in this world," because I felt it was my duty to be as much like Him as possible in this world. But the definite statement that, "As he is, so *are* we in this world" was more than I could take in, until light from heaven shone upon this passage and I saw that what He was speaking about was not exactly our personal experience, or our personal growth in grace, or our likeness to Christ in that way; but it was our justification before God, our acceptance in the Beloved. In that sense, God sees every believer in Christ. As He is, so are we before God down here in this world.

That is what is involved in the Epistle to the Romans, chapter 8: "There is therefore now no condemnation to them which are in Christ Jesus." I am in Him before the Father. He sees me in His Son and I have a perfect, a complete standing in Christ. Every believer is made meet to be a partaker "of the inheritance of the saints in light."

But now in verse 9 of Second Corinthians, chapter 5, the apostle says, "Wherefore we labour, that, whether present or absent, we may be accepted of him." Notice "accepted *of* him," not accepted *in* him. "Accepted of him" means well pleasing to Him. Now he is referring to our behaviour, to our practical experience, to our service; and he says, "We are labouring, we are working now, we are ambitious to be well-pleasing to Him. We want his approbation day by day." I want the approval of the Lord; don't you? I can hardly conceive of a Christian who does not desire that his life be pleasing to God.

And then he goes on to say, "For we must all appear," we must all be manifested, "before the judgment seat of Christ." The day is coming when we are going to leave this scene. The Lord is coming back for His own, and the dead shall be raised and the living changed. Then we shall appear at His judgment seat. Somebody may say, "How do you know that this judgment seat of Christ is just subsequent to the rapture of the Church?" Well, in the book of the Revelation, the last chapter, we get this: "Behold, I come quickly; and my reward is with me, to give every man according as his work shall be" (22:12). You see, when He comes again, when He returns for His own, His reward will be with Him. The judgment seat of Christ is the place where we shall be manifested in order that we may receive our reward. And so the apostle says, "We must all," we believers—he is speaking of the two classes, the resurrected dead and the living who shall be changed—"We must all appear before the judgment seat of Christ."

Somebody has suggested that the original word here has really the thought of a complete opening up, a complete unveiling, and it might be translated, "We shall all be turned inside out at the judgment seat of Christ." How would you like to be turned inside out now? How would you like to have all your thoughts made manifest? all your hidden motives? I think that would be rather humbling for some of us.

There is more hypocrisy about many of us than we would like to let people know. Of course, if people knew, then it would no longer be hypocrisy. We may do some covering up now, but the day is coming when it will all be made manifest. One may pretend to be humble and lowly and to seek the will of the Lord, and all the time in the heart there is envy and strife and jealousy of others, and one does not like to see other people recognized in place of oneself.

Oh, if we were turned inside out now, I think there would be some tremendous showings up! Friends would see a lot of things that many of them never dreamed were hidden away in the heart. Well, we ought to be real, we ought to seek to be genuine, because it is all coming out some day. The Lord Jesus has told us that everything is going to be made manifest in that coming day. Every idle word and the thoughts of the heart are going to be made known. "We must all be made manifest before the judgment seat of Christ."

And let me say this. The judgment seat of Christ, as we have it here, should not be confounded with the judgment of the great white throne at the end of the world. Now, of course, the great white throne will be Christ's judgment seat also. He said, "The Father judgeth no man, but hath committed all judgment unto the Son" (John 5:22). So when the wicked dead are raised at the end of time and they stand before the great white throne, do you know who will be seated on that throne? The same blessed One who suffered once to save them, and from whom they have turned away. They will behold seated on the throne of judgment the Man who hung on Calvary's cross, the Lord Jesus Christ, for He is God as well as Man. God is going to judge the world, but He is going to judge the world in the person of His Son.

The judgment of the great white throne, of which we read in Revelation 20, is the judgment of the wicked. The judgment seat of Christ is a different type of judgment altogether. It is the judgment of God's beloved people when they come before Him to give an account of their lives since He saved them. They are not going there to be judged for their sins, because these have all been put away by the precious blood of Christ; but they are going there to give an account of their service, and the Lord will take cognizance of all that His people have done, whether it has been good or bad, whether it has been the work of the flesh or the work of the Spirit; "that every one may receive the things done in his body, according to that he hath done, whether it be good or bad" (II Cor. 5:10).

It will be a very wonderful time when we stand there in our glorified bodies. You see, we will not go there to find out whether we are going to heaven, but we will be there glorified in our resurrection bodies. It will be a very wonderful time when we stand there before our blessed Lord and He says, "Now I am going to show you how all of your works appeared to me." To many of us it will be a tremendous revelation. We have worked hard and laboured long, and sometimes we have been so discouraged and felt as though we had not accomplished anything; and then the Lord is going to open things up and say, "You remember the time when you were so disheartened? You just felt that you were working away and your ministry wasn't counting for anything, but at that very time this precious soul was brought to know Christ." That night when you were so discouraged and you felt that you were such a failure as a preacher, and you told the Lord that perhaps you didn't belong in the ministry at all, you will find at the judgment seat of Christ that the Lord used that message to lead some soul to Himself.

We have those experiences here on earth sometimes. I remember one time I had prayed so earnestly for a meeting, and I spent so much time before God and my expectation was great. I just poured my heart out in the message that night, but there was no response at all. Nobody seemed to be interested, and I did not even try to get down to the door to meet anybody, I felt so discouraged. So I slipped out the back way and went home and threw myself down on my knees and cried out to the Lord, telling Him what a complete failure I was and that nobody got any blessing. I was so utterly disheartened! Then about three months later I was leaving that place after having worked on for nine months in all, and I got a letter from a young woman who had been singing in the choir.

She wrote me and said, "I have never told you of my salvation, and I feel that before you go I ought to tell you." She gave me the exact date. She said it was so vivid in her mind that she would never forget it. "I was singing in the choir that night. In fact," she said, "I sang a solo. You know, I always thought I was a Christian, but that night God revealed my own heart to me. I saw that I had never been converted, and when you asked for anybody who wanted to receive Christ to come to Him then, I had such an urge to walk down to the platform and publicly confess Christ, but I was ashamed. I went home so miserable, so wretched; but thank God, before I retired I broke down before Him. I got down on my knees and confessed my sins and took Christ as my Saviour, and everything has been so different since. I have never had the courage to tell you before, but I felt that I must tell you before you left."

I checked up and found that it was that night when I was so utterly discouraged. That night God had wrought a miracle in that young woman's life.

I think there will be many things like that in the day of manifestation. I think the Lord will show many of us how He used the Word, when we did not know He was using it at all. Or just the manner of life lived will have borne fruit in someone's life, and at the judgment seat of Christ that one will say, "I watched that man, that woman, at their work; I watched them when things went wrong, and they manifested such a kind, gracious spirit. I watched to see if they would get angry or upset when their wishes were crossed, but they were so meek and so gracious and so Christianlike. I said to myself, 'There is something there I would give a great deal to have.' That message led me to Christ. I have never told them, but I am telling them now."

Many things are going to come out like that, and for everything that has been done for Christ, there will be rewards. But there will be the other side of it. I am afraid many of us will be disappointed in that day. So much of our service has been done in the energy of the flesh, and we shall be disappointed when the Lord has to say to us, "Your life hasn't counted very much for me. You were so much concerned with magnifying yourself, with building up your own reputation, with what people would think of you, and you just fattened on applause and praise. Well, you have had your reward. I do not have any for you now. You had it all down there. You will have to suffer loss. You did not work for my glory; you were not concerned about making me known. You were concerned about your own reputation. You wanted people to speak well of you. Well, you have had your success, but there is no reward for you here."

He is coming!  Oh, how solemn!
When the Judge's voice is heard,
And in His own light He shows us
Every thought and act and word!
Deeds of merit, as we thought them,
He will show us were but sin;
Little acts we had forgotten,
He will tell us were for Him.

It will be a wonderful thing to get His mind about it all, but a very solemn thing, too.

Now turn back to that passage in the first Epistle to the Corinthians, chapter 3. These Corinthians were making a great deal of Christian leaders, so much so that they were actually dividing themselves, sectarianly. One of them would say, "I am of Paul," another would say, "I am of Apollos," and still another would say, "I am of Cephas." I don't know that they used the actual names. I really don't think they did, because the sixth verse of the fourth chapter, it seems to me, negatives that:

> And these things, brethren, I have in a figure transferred to myself and to Apollos for your sakes; that ye might learn in us not to think of men above that which is written, that no one of you be puffed up for one against another. For who maketh thee to differ from another? and what hast thou that thou didst not receive? now if thou didst receive it, why dost thou glory, as if thou hadst not received it? (I Corinthians 4:6, 7).

You see, "I have transferred these things in a figure to myself and to Apollos." What probably was taking place was this:

Some were saying, "I enjoy a man like Paul who really teaches the Word. I do not care to go and hear these light-weights. I like a man who digs down under the letter and gives us something weighty." Another says, "I haven't much use for that dry as dust Bible teacher. He is too deep for me. I like a man who can soar up into the clouds. I enjoy one who can preach with unction and liberty, an eloquent man, and a man mighty in the Scriptures. Give me Apollos! I like to hear a great preacher. I am not interested in going to church when somebody is just expounding the Bible. I want something that thrills me." Another says, "I like the exhorter. I like the man who gets down to something practical and stirs you up, and makes you feel your own need and the importance of Christian living. I am not interested in Bible teaching or in eloquent preaching. I like good, faithful exhortation. I am of Cephas."

But the apostle says, "They have all received their gifts of the Lord, and the gifts are for the whole Church. Do not under-value one and put the other on a pedestal. Thank God for them all. There are some times when you need the Bible teacher; there are times when you need the eloquent preacher; and there are times when you need the exhorter. Thank God for every one of them." See what he says:

> Who then is Paul, and who is Apollos, but ministers by whom ye believed, even as the Lord gave to every man? I have planted, Apollos watered; but God gave the increase. So then neither is he that planteth any thing, neither he that watereth; but God that giveth the increase (I Corinthians 3:5-7).

In other words, don't make too much of the instrument. It is God who gives the increase, and whether he works through the teacher or the preacher or the exhorter, you just give Him the glory; give Him the praise.

Then as to the laborer, "He that planteth and he that watereth are one," and he has already said that they are both nothing; so they are just men, both of them. They do not amount to anything in themselves, but "every man shall receive his own reward according to his own labour" (verse 8). There you have it! That is the reward that Christians are to receive at the judgment seat of Christ. You do your work faithfully in the place that God has put you and do not be worried because you cannot do what someone else is doing. You will get your reward. There is no need to be jealous; there is no need to be envious because someone else gets more recognition than you do. Do that which God has commanded you, and do it as unto the Lord. Each shall receive his own reward according to his own labour.

> Ye are God's husbandry, ye are God's building. According to the grace of God which is given unto me, as a wise master-builder, . . . (I Corinthians 3:9, 10).

Paul had gone into Corinth and laid out the plans for the work, and was used of God to establish the church there.

> I have laid the foundation, and another buildeth thereupon. But let every man take heed how he buildeth thereupon. For other foundation can no man lay than that is laid, which is Jesus Christ (vv. 10, 11).

The Church rests upon Christ, and Christ alone.

"Now if any man build upon this foundation"—he is on the Foundation; he is in Christ. Now he is building: "Gold, silver, precious stones. . . " These will glorify God. They speak of that which is precious in His sight.

But then there are "wood, hay, stubble." These speak of that which is worthless; they will never abide the test of judgment fire.

"Every man's work shall be made manifest." This tells us that everything will come out in that day:

> For the day shall declare it, because it shall be revealed by fire.

The fire of God's holiness will test every man's work. Will it come up to God's standard? Will it come up to what He has a right to expect? He is going to test it! "The fire shall try every man's work of what sort it is."

It is a great comfort to me to know that it does not say, "How *much* it is." All my life there has been so much I have wanted to do; there have been so many, many places I should like to go and preach; there are so many things I wish I could accomplish for Christ, but time and strength make it impossible. As I look back over the years, I have been able to do so little compared with what I might have done; but I get a lot of comfort out of this scripture: "Every man's work shall be made manifest: for the day shall declare it, because it shall be revealed by fire; and the fire shall try every man's work of *what sort* it is." And my heart says. "O Lord, help me to do the right sort of work, even if I can't do a great deal. God give me to do the right sort—the work that is the result of the control of the Holy Spirit in my life, in accordance with the Word of God."

> If any man's work abide which he hath built thereupon, he shall receive a reward (v. 14).

This is not salvation; this is reward! You say, "Well, do you work for a reward?" We work for the glory of God, but He delights to give rewards.

I attended a men's banquet at one of our city churches one night, where I was to speak, and they had just been doing a good deal of building and in a very nice way they were recognizing the different men who had accomplished quite a little in their program. One dear aged brother was called to the front, and they said something like this: "He has probably done more for the work of the church on this occasion than almost anyone else," and they wanted to give him a gift. He came forward quite diffidently and said, "What I did, I did for the Lord. I was not looking for any thanks and I was not looking for any gift, but since you have been so kind and have done this for me, I accept your gift and thank you for it."

I think that is the way we will speak to the Lord when He says, "Now, you did this for me, and you did that and you did the other, and now I want to reward you. I am going to give you a crown of righteousness, or a crown of glory." I think we shall feel like saying, "Blessed Lord, I did not do that for a reward; I did it for Thee because I love Thee. But since in Thy rich grace Thou delightest to give rewards, I receive it as from Thyself and thank Thee for it."

In the day of manifestation! And I think we shall feel ashamed, if we have nothing for which we may be rewarded.

> If any man's work shall be burned (if all his work seems to go for nothing), he shall suffer loss (v. 15).

This will have nothing to do with the question of his eternal salvation, for we read:

> But he himself shall be saved; yet so as by fire.

God grant that each one of us may serve faithfully in view of that day of manifestation, and that we may have a rich reward because of heart devotion to Christ down here!

# GLORIFICATION

For as many as are led by the Spirit of God, they are the sons of God. For ye have not received the spirit of bondage again to fear; but ye have received the Spirit of adoption, whereby we cry, Abba, Father. The Spirit himself beareth witness with our spirit, that we are the children of God: and if children, then heirs; heirs of God, and joint-heirs with Christ; if so be that we suffer with him, that we may be also *glorified* together . . . And we know that all things work together for good to them that love God, to them who are the called according to his purpose. For whom he did foreknow, he also did predestinate to be conformed to the image of his Son, that he might be the firstborn among many brethren. Moreover whom he did predestinate, them he also called: and whom he called, them he also justified: and whom he justified, them he also glorified (Romans 8:14-17; 28-30).

HAVE you ever tried to define the word *glory?* It has always seemed to me to be one of the most difficult words in the English language to explain. We read a great deal about glory in the Bible, but just what is meant when that term is used? Sometimes, of course, it is used in the sense of boastfulness. "My soul shall make her boast in the Lord," and that is a boastfulness that is perfectly right. And so we are told, "Let him that glorieth, glory in the Lord." We are warned against vain glory, against glorying in our own strength, or in our own fancied wisdom. But the word *glory* is used in a great many other senses in the Bible.

Our Lord Jesus prayer, "Glorify thou me with thine own self with the glory which I had with thee before the world was," and there He was referring to the splendor of deity which He left in order to come down into this world, veiling His deity in humanity. Even when He was here on earth, we are told by the apostle John, "We beheld his glory, the glory as of the only begotten of the Father, full of grace and truth." It is very difficult to put in other words the exact meaning of that expression. What does it mean to you—"We beheld his glory"? We connect with the word sometimes the thought of resplendence, brilliance, like the glory of the sunshine, whether of the rising sun or the setting sun. But when John wrote, "We beheld his glory," he was not referring to anything like that. On the Mount of Transfiguration they saw that kind of glory. He appeared in glory—bright, shining, brilliant—His raiment white and glistening, whiter than any fuller on earth could possibly have made it. But what was that glory of which John spoke, "We beheld his glory?" It was the beauty of His intrinsic character. They saw in that lowly Man the glory of deity shining out, the glory of His divine character seen shining through the veil of His humanity.

But when Scripture speaks of the glory that awaits us, what does that mean? We think of heaven as a place of brilliance, a place of marvelous beauty, and yet that is not exactly the thought that is connected with glory and with our glorification. Among a great many different definitions which the dictionary gives for *glory* I have selected these as fitting, it seems to me, more definitely than others with what I have in mind. Glory means honor, distinction, that of which we may rightfully boast, brilliancy, splendor, radiant beauty; and then I am so glad that Webster says, "celestial bliss," for that after all is the glory that is before us.

Now Scripture links our coming glory with our present suffering. We read here in Romans 8:14-17, that if we suffer with Him, we may also be glorified together. It is not telling us that our glory is absolutely dependent on our suffering, and that we will only be glorified provided we have suffered to some certain extent, but it is telling us that the glory that is coming will fully repay us for any suffering that we may endure for Christ's sake down here. And notice in this instance it does not say, "If we suffer *for* him," but, "If we suffer *with* him, we shall be glorified together."

You who have recently come to Christ, you who are young in the Christian life, you have already begun to realize that it is impossible to be a consistent Christian without to some extent suffering with Him who has saved you. The Lord Jesus Christ is still unpopular.

> Our Lord is now rejected
> And by the world disowned,
> By the many still neglected
> And by the few enthroned.
> But soon He'll come in glory,
> The hour is drawing nigh,
> For the crowning day is coming
> By and by.

He has said to us, "Ye are not of the world, even as I am not of the world. Marvel not then if the world hate you. If the world hate you, remember it hated me before it hated you." If I am going to take my stand as a witness for Christ in the world that has rejected Him, of very necessity it entails a certain amount of suffering. I cannot look for the approval of the world. I must expect to bear a measure, at least, of reproach and shame for Christ's name's sake.

But after all, to suffer *with* Him is something different from suffering *for* Him. I suffer for Him when I stand out for His name's sake and bear witness to His testimony, enduring positive persecution if the world chooses to turn against me. But every believer suffers *with* Christ as he finds his spirit oppressed and troubled because of conditions prevailing all about him. How could I be a Christian and live in any sense in fellowship with the Lord

Jesus Christ and not suffer as I go through this evil world?
A poet has written:

> Saddened, ah yes, saddened
> By earth's deep sin and woe.
> How could I pass unheeding
> What grieved my Saviour so?

We suffer as we see men for whom Christ died spurning
His grace, trampling on His love, and in spite of every
effort put forth for their salvation, ruthlessly rushing on to
eternal judgment. It fills our hearts with pain. It causes
intense suffering. The more we think of it and the more
we realize what it means, the keener the suffering.

The apostle Paul says of servants of Christ that we are a
sweet savour unto God, both in them that are saved and in
them that perish. I shall never forget kneeling one time
with a brother evangelist as we were about to go into an
evening meeting, and suddenly my friend burst into a
passion of tears and broke out in prayer something like
this: "O Lord, do grant tonight that as we go to the platform to proclaim Thy Word we may not be a savour of
death unto death, but of life unto life. So often we preach
Thy Word and men turn coldly away, and instead of the
world coming to it for blessing, it only increases their
condemnation. O God," he pleaded, "may it not be so
tonight." And I think every lover of souls can understand
his feeling.

Richard Baxter used to pray from the depths of a heart
breaking over the sins of a lost world, "O God, for a full
heaven and an empty hell." But alas, alas, that prayer
cannot be answered because men will persist in trampling
on the love and grace of the Saviour who came to redeem
them. As a true Christian contemplates this, he suffers. It
cannot be otherwise. As he sees the pain and the sorrow
that men are enduring because of sin, he suffers as Christ

suffered. Our Lord groaned in the spirit and was troubled when He saw the ravages that death had made; and so the Christian suffers as he sees that which comes upon mankind because of sin.

But, thank God, the day is coming when the reward will answer in the fullest possible sense to all present suffering. "If so be that we suffer with him, that we may be also glorified together." When He shines forth in glory, then we shall shine forth in the same glory with Him, since it is for this that God has saved us.

Look again at that golden chain in verses 29 and 30, reaching from the eternity in the past to the glorious eternity in the future:

> For whom he did foreknow, he also did predestinate to be conformed to the image of his Son, that he might be the firstborn among many brethren. Moreover whom he did predestinate, them he also called: and whom he called, them he also justified: and whom he justified, them he also *glorified*.

See these golden links that join the ages before creation to the ages to come when this world, this lower universe, will have passed away:

> Divine foreknowledge
> Divine predestination
> Divine calling
> Divine justification
> Divine glorification.

God knew you, my brother, my sister, long before you ever came into existence. He knew every sin you would be guilty of. He knew every failure that would mark your life, and knowing it all, He marked you out as an object of His grace. In His foreknowledge He saw the moment when you, as a poor sinner, would turn to God confessing your guilt and would put your trust in Christ. Also, He has predestinated you to be conformed to the image of His Son. Do not get the wrong idea when you read in the Bible about predestination. Do not allow any thoughts of fatalistic philosophy to bewilder your mind. Remember this: nowhere in Scripture are we told that God predestined anybody to go to heaven, and certainly we never read that He predestinated anybody to go to hell. Predestination is never linked up either with heaven or with hell, as such.

What does God predestinate people for? He predestinates those whom He foreknew to be conformed to the image of His Son. Ah, dear young Christian, have you already begun to get discouraged with yourself sometimes, and do you weep in secret over sins that you know have dishonored your Lord? Those are grateful tears and He appreciates them, and you may rest upon the Word, "If we confess our sins, he is faithful and just to forgive us our sins, and to cleanse us from all unrighteousness." But do not let any degrees of failure ever fill your heart with discouragement. Remember that God has predestinated you to become some day just like the Lord Jesus Christ. That is what predestination means. He has predestinated you to eventual holiness, to eventual perfection, morally and spiritually, and it is for this purpose that He has called you by His grace. He called you through the message of the gospel, and mark, He knew everything you would be before He called you at all. I have had people say to me sometimes, when they come to consult me about some failure in their lives, "Oh, I feel God must be so disappointed in me." Let me tell you something. God has never been disappointed in any of us. He knew just how foolish we were going to be, just how we would fail, before He took us up. And yet He called us by His grace.

And whom He called, them He also justified. And to be justified, as we have already seen in this series of messages, is to be cleared of every charge, so that God absolutely refuses to listen to any accusation brought against any of His blood-redeemed people. We are "justified freely by his grace through the redemption that is in Christ Jesus"; and this justification is not changed by fluctuations in our spiritual experience. You all know the old camp meeting song:

> I'm sometimes up, and sometimes down,
> But still my soul *feels* heavenly bound."
> It might better be rendered:
> I'm sometimes up, and sometimes down,
> But still my soul *is* heavenly bound.

For if you have been justified before God, He says, "Who is he that condemneth? It is Christ that died, yea rather, that is risen again, who is even at the right hand of God, who also maketh intercession for us."

See what completes the chain: "Whom he justified, them he also *glorified*." Now do get that straight, young believer. It does not say, "Some of those whom he justified, he also glorified." It does not say, "Those who were once justified and kept holding on to the end were eventually justified." It says, "Whom he justified, them he also *glorified*." When God justifies a man, He saves him for eternity, and He will never be through with him until He has him in the same glory with Christ.

Some people have a very strange idea as to the meaning of God's salvation. That salvation is beautifully illustrated away back in the Old Testament. You remember when God was about to bring the flood of judgment upon the earth, He commanded Noah to build an ark for the saving of his house. Then when the ark was all completed, God said to Him, "Come thou and all thy house into the ark." When they entered the ark, they were safe there until the judgment was passed, until in God's due time they came out upon a new earth.

I have often tried to illustrate the ideas some people have of God's salvation by putting it like this; suppose that after the work was completed the word of the Lord came to Noah saying, "Now, Noah, I want you to go and get eight good, big, strong spikes." Noah says, "Eight spikes, Lord?" "Yes, I want you to get eight good, big, strong spikes." So Noah goes off and gets these spikes. Then the Lord says, "I want you to drive these into the side of the ark, a reasonable distance apart, and leave enough of them outside in order that one may hold on to them." Noah drives them into the side of the ark. Then imagine the voice of the Lord saying to Noah, "Come now, and all thy house, and hang on to these spikes, and it shall come to pass that whosoever shall hang on to these spikes until the flood is over will eventually be saved"! Would not that be a poor kind of salvation? I can imagine Noah getting hold of one spike and Mrs. Noah getting hold of another spike, and Japheth grasps his spike and Mrs. Japheth her spike, and Shem and Ham and their wives theirs—each one hanging on; and then Noah trying to encourage them by saying, "Now, my dear sons, my dear wife, my dear daughters-in-law, I want you all to make up your minds that no matter what comes, you are going to hold on to the very end, for if you do, you'll get through all right; if you let go, you will be lost in the flood waters."

Then just imagine the rains descending and the floods rising, and the old ark beginning to shiver and quiver and rise upon the face of the deep, and there are the eight hanging onto their spikes for dear life. It would not be long until Noah would cry out, "Mama, how are you getting along?" and she would reply, "Noah, I'm holding on; do pray that I may hold on to the end." And each one would put in a similar plea. By and by the weakest one of the crowd, perhaps, I don't know which one, would cry out, "Oh, it seems as if I can't hold on any longer," and would let go and be carried away in the flood. How long do you think it would be until they all would be carried away, if it depended on their hanging on?

That was not God's way. He said, "Noah, Come thou and all thy house into the ark," and they went in and the Lord shut them in, and they did not get out until the renewed earth lay there in all its beauty before them. Then they were able to go forth as worshippers.

When God justifies a sinner, that sinner is in Christ; and there is no condemnation to those who are in Christ Jesus. It is true that inside the ark order should prevail. I have no doubt that Noah and his family all sought to behave themselves inside the ark as those who owed everything to the matchless grace of God which had delivered them. So you and I should devote all our lives and powers to the glory of Him who has saved us. But our salvation does not depend upon our devotedness and faithfulness. It depends upon *His* faithfulness. "He is faithful who hath promised."

And now the end: "Whom he justified, them he also *glorified*." If you have trusted Christ, you can look on to the glory; and when that glory comes, it will repay you for everything you ever had to endure in the way of trial and sorrow in this poor world.

Look at Second Corinthians, chapter 4, verses 17 and 18:

> For our light affliction, which is but for a moment, worketh for us a far more exceeding and eternal weight of glory; while we look not at the things which are seen, but at the things which are not seen: for the things which are seen are temporal; but the things which are not seen are eternal.

Are you disposed, perhaps, to raise a question here and say, "Well, Paul by the Spirit speaks there of our light affliction which is but for a moment, but my affliction has been very heavy, and instead of being for a moment, it has already lasted for weary months or years." Ah, but wait a moment, dear friend. Granting all that, then it ought to give you a greater conception of what the glory is going to be when you are finally at home with Christ, because there awaits you a far more exceeding and eternal weight of glory. Notice the contrast here. God calls your present affliction "light," though it may seem to you very heavy; but it is light as contrasted with the weight of glory that is coming. It may seem sometimes, dear troubled soul, as though you cannot bear any more, but your Father is taking note of everything and He is going to repay in His own wonderful way when you see His face, by giving you far more yonder than you ever could possibly have entered into in your thoughts down here.

Let the apostle Peter add a word to this. In his first Epistle, chapter 1, he writes to encourage suffering, troubled saints:

> Wherein ye greatly rejoice, though now for a season, if need be, ye are in heaviness through manifold temptations: that the trial of your faith, being much more precious than of gold that perisheth, though it be tried with fire, might be found unto praise and honour and glory at the appearing of Jesus Christ: whom having not seen, ye love; in whom, though now ye see him not, yet believing, ye rejoice with joy unspeakable and full of glory: receiving the end of your faith, even the salvation of our souls (verses 6 to 9).

Whatever you are going through in the way of heart-break, bereavement, sickness, financial distress, trouble in the family, trouble in the church, trouble in the world—whatever you are called upon to endure that is testing your heart and mind to the very breaking point, remember it is but like the fire that is purifying the gold, and when God gets through there will be only the pure gold left. Your faith will be found then unto praise and honor and glory at the appearing of Jesus Christ.

In the fourth chapter of this same Epistle, Peter speaks again of trial and glory. He says in verses 12 and 13:

> Beloved, think it not strange concerning the fiery trail which is to try you, as though some strange thing happened unto you: but rejoice, inasmuch as ye are partakers of Christ's sufferings; that, when his glory shall be revealed, ye may be glad also with exceeding joy.

Partakers of Christ's suffering! He suffered down in this scene. He has been glorified up yonder, and you and I are going to share His glory.

In the seventeenth chapter of John we have recorded Christ's prayer to the Father in our behalf. He says, "Father, the glory which thou hast given me, I have given them." And then He expresses His delight that the day is coming when they shall behold His glory. Do you remember when Joseph had been sold as a slave by his heartless brothers, and then was purchased by Potiphar and afterwards knew long, weary months and possibly years in prison, and was finally brought to stand before Pharaoh and became the deliverer of his world in his day? He sent for his brothers and his father, and said, "I want them to come to me that they may behold my glory." You get some idea of what the Lord Jesus meant when He said, "I will that they also, whom thou hast given me, be with me where I am; that they may behold my glory."

We shall behold the glory of Him who was once rejected down here—now glorified, honored of the Father, and we shall share the glory that came to Him because of His suffering, because of what He endured for the Father's sake, and in order to work out His redemption for us in this scene. What a prospect we have before us! "Whom he justified, them he also *glorified.*"

# The Moody Colportage Library

## GOSPEL STORIES

## BIOGRAPHY

---

**MOODY PRESS, Chicago 10, Illinois • 35c each**

# The Moody Colportage Library

## SALVATION

## CHILDREN'S BOOKS

MOODY PRESS, Chicago 10, Illinois • 35c each

# The Moody Colportage Library

## BETTER CHRISTIAN LIFE

**MOODY PRESS**, Chicago 10, Illinois • 35c each

# The Moody Colportage Library

## PRAYER

## BIBLE STUDY

**MOODY PRESS**, Chicago 10, Illinois • 35c each